CLASS MANAGEMENT

Successful teachers operate in many different ways, but they have one thing in common – an ability to manage their classrooms effectively. Without this basic skill, the most inspiring and knowledgeable teacher will fail.

In *Class Management*, Ted Wragg helps teachers to clarify their own aims and to find the strategies which will work for them. Topics covered include first encounters, the establishment of rules and relationships, management of time and space and specific discipline problems.

Ted Wragg is head of the school of education at Exeter University and the author of many books including *Classroom Teaching Skills* and, with John Partington, *A Handbook for School Governors*. He writes a regular column for the *Times Educational Supplement* and is a frequent commentator for radio and television on education matters.

Clive Carré is co-ordinator of the Leverhulme Primary Project and series editor for the *Classroom Skills* series. He has taught science at primary and secondary levels and has written and acted as a consultant on science materials in the UK, Australia and Canada.

LEVERHULME PRIMARY PROJECT

The Leverhulme Primary project, based at Exeter University, directed by Ted Wragg and Neville Bennett and co-ordinated by Clive Carré is a major survey of primary teacher education since 1988. Its bank of valuable information about what actually happens in classrooms and how teachers are reacting to current changes in education will be used for a variety of publications including the *Classroom Skills* series and a series on the teaching of individual subjects in the National Curriculum.

LEVERHULME PRIMARY PROJECT ■ *Classroom Skills series*

All primary teachers need to master certain basic pedagogical skills. This set of innovative yet practical resource books for teachers covers each of those skills in turn. Each book contains

- Practical, written and oral activities for individual and group use at all stages of professional development
- Transcripts of classroom conversation and teacher feedback and photographs of classroom practice to stimulate discussion
- Succinct and practical explanatory text

Other titles in the series

TALKING AND LEARNING IN GROUPS   *Elisabeth Dunne and Neville Bennett*
EXPLAINING   *E.C. Wragg and George Brown*
QUESTIONING   *George Brown and E.C.Wragg*
EFFECTIVE TEACHING   *E.C.Wragg*

Leverhulme Primary Project ■ Classroom Skills Series

Series editor
Clive Carré

CLASS MANAGEMENT

E.C.Wragg

London and New York

First published 1993
by Routledge
11 New Fetter Lane, London EC4P 4EE

Simultaneously published in the USA and Canada
by Routledge
29 West 35th Street, New York, NY 10001

© 1993 E.C. Wragg

Filmset in Palatino by Selwood Systems, Midsomer Norton
Printed and bound in Great Britain by Butler & Tanner Ltd,
Frome and London

British Library Cataloguing in Publication Data

A catalogue record for this book is available from the British
Library.

ISBN 0–415–08422–9

Library of Congress Cataloging in Publication Data

Library of Congress Cataloging in Publication data has been
applied for.

ISBN 0–415–08422–9

CONTENTS

PREFACE

Improving the quality of what happens in primary school and preparing children for life in the twenty-first century requires the highest quality of professional training. The Leverhulme Primary Project *Classroom Skills* Series and its companion series *Curriculum in Primary Practice* are designed to assist in this training.

The Leverhulme Primary Project Classroom Skills Series focuses on the essential classroom competences. It explores the classroom strategies available to teachers and the patterns of classroom organization which best assist pupil learning. Throughout, it demonstrates that at the very heart of teacher education is the ability to make sense of what is going on in the classroom. This series of books is based on the research of the Leverhulme Primary Project, a three-year programme of research into various aspects of primary teacher education, funded by the Leverhulme Trust and carried out at the University of Exeter. The companion series, *Curriculum in Primary Practice* helps teachers to make judgements and devise strategies for teaching particular subjects.

Both series are designed to assist teachers at all stages of their professional development. They will be useful for:
- practising teachers
- student teachers
- college and university tutors
- school-based in-service co-ordinators
- advisory teachers
- school mentors and headteachers.

This book can be used as part of initial training or in in-service programmes in school. The text can also be read by individuals as a source of ideas and it will be helpful in teacher appraisal as an aid to developing professional awareness both for those being appraised and for the appraisers. Like all the books in both series, *Class Management* contains suggested activities which have been tried out by teachers and those in pre-service training and revised in the light of their comments.

We hope that both series will provoke discussion, help you to reflect on your current practice and encourage you to ask questions about everyday classroom events.

Clive Carré,
University of Exeter

ACKNOWLEDGEMENTS

My thanks to Allyson Trotter and Caroline Wragg who did much of the fieldwork on class management in the Leverhulme Primary Project, and to Barbara Janssen who analysed some of the data.

AIMS AND CONTENT

Without the ability to manage a class effectively, any other skills teachers have may be neutralized. It is no good knowing your subject matter, being able to devise interesting activities appropriate to the topic, knowing what sort of questions to ask or being able to give a clear explanation, if you cannot obtain a hearing or organize a group of children.

The principal aim of this book, therefore, is to give newcomers to the profession some basic notions and precepts about class management, and also to allow experienced teachers to examine their own practice and, it is hoped, improve it. One of the most satisfying features of teaching is that it is possible to work at and improve professional skills throughout one's teaching career. The ideas in the six units are in part based on our own research into classroom management and that of others, and the activities have been tried out and evaluated over several years.

The intention is that, by reading the text and trying out some of the practical activities, teachers will be able to improve their own classroom practice. The emphasis is on both activity and reflection, for one without the other would be less effective. All the activities can be done by individuals or by groups of student or experienced teachers, either in discussion or with children on their own or in someone else's classroom. The use of jargon is minimized, though not omitted entirely. For example, Jacob Kounin's use of terms such as 'withitness' (meaning 'having eyes in the back of your head' or being aware of what is going on in various parts of the classroom) is kept, as these are graphic terms easily remembered.

The book is organized in the following six units.

In **Unit 1** there is an analysis of what constitutes effective class management.
Unit 2 describes and explores the different philosophies and approaches to class management.

Unit 3 explores the very first encounters that teachers have with a new class.
Unit 4 deals with the two Rs, rules and relationships.
Unit 5 concentrates on decision-making, including the handling of deviant and disruptive behaviour.
Unit 6 looks ahead to the development of greater competence in class management.

There is no favouring of a single approach to class management, therefore. The emphasis is on teachers exploring the issues, considering alternatives, trying out ideas and then finding their own best way forward in the light of their own experience and that of others.

How to use this book

The six units constitute substantial course material in class management. The activities and text are suitable for in-service and professional studies courses as well as for individual use.

The text may be read as a book in its own right; all the *activities* can be undertaken either by individual teachers or by members of a group working together on the topic.

The discussion activities can be used in group meetings, for example, or as part of staff discussion during a school's INSET day. The individual reader can use these as a prompt for reflection and planning.

The written activities are intended to be worked on individually but also lend themselves to group discussion when completed.

The practical activities are designed to be done in the teacher's own classroom or by student teachers on teaching practice or when they are teaching children brought into the training institution for professional work.

The book can either be used alone or in conjunction

with other books in the Classroom Skills series. For example, the management of small groups is not covered in great detail because the book by Elisabeth Dunne and Neville Bennett, *Talking and Learning in Groups*, in the Classroom Skills series covers the topic much more fully.

Those responsible for courses, therefore, may well wish to put together exercises and activities from several of the books in this series to make up their own course as part of a general professional skills development programme, either in initial training or of whole school professional development. Usually the discussion and written activities described will occupy between 1 and $1\frac{1}{2}$ hours and classroom activities may be completed in about half an hour, though this may vary, depending on the context.

The following symbols are used throughout the book to denote:

quotations from published materials

activities

transcripts of children or teachers talking during lessons

SKILFUL CLASS MANAGEMENT

If you watch primary-age children playing together at home or in school, before long someone will suggest playing at 'school'. At the beginning of this time-honoured fantasy game a common ritual is followed. One child will step forward and say, 'I'll be the teacher' and from then onwards that person is assumed to be in charge. There is not usually a rush to say, 'Bags I be the rather quiet child who sits in a corner getting on obediently with some number work', but then children are not prone to use adult language in these matters.

It is fascinating to see what happens next. Some children role-playing as a teacher will immediately move centre stage and start ordering everyone else around, 'Right, you sit here, you go over there'. It seems to be the element of control that attracts. Others mimic a more kindly style. In this mirror of classroom life, where the players know better than anyone else what the reality is, some children will start to misbehave and then may be told off or even sometimes whacked about the body or head in a way that would have a real teacher up before the nearest magistrate.

Control over the behaviour of others, however, is only one aspect of class management. Every day, busy primary teachers will find they are planning lessons; choosing topics or tasks; making judgements about what they as teachers should determine and what children should be encouraged to decide or choose for themselves; supervising movement around the classroom or school; organizing often a variety of activities undertaken by individuals, small groups (see the workbook *Talking and Learning in Groups* by Elisabeth Dunne and Neville Bennett in this Routledge series) or the whole class; praising good work or reprimanding pupils who misbehave; making sure the right materials and books are available; selecting from a range of possible teaching strategies. All these are aspects of class management and the list could go on.

The importance of effective class management is well illustrated by the following true story. A few years ago I was external examiner at a college in London. This involved visiting students on teaching practice, seeing them teach and discussing with their tutors and supervising teachers in the schools whether they should pass or fail. I arrived at a primary school and was met by the head. She told me that the student had had considerable discipline problems, had not been able to control one or two of the more difficult pupils and, in her view, should not be allowed to pass. I spent the morning watching the student concerned and was surprised at how orderly the class actually was. The lesson was quite interesting, pupils got on with their work and there did not seem to be too much difference between this student and others who were in the lower band of the pass category.

The sequel, however, was that, when I spoke to the student, she confessed her surprise at the good behaviour of the class and the relative smoothness of the lesson. Her teaching practice had gone very badly, she explained, because of poor behaviour by the pupils, and she fully expected to fail. Indeed, this was the first lesson for weeks that had gone according to plan and in a civilized manner. When I explained to the head what had happened she could not at first believe it. Suddenly she had an idea. 'Let me talk to Jane', she said.

Five minutes later she returned and all became clear. Jane was the kind-hearted deputy head who normally taught the student's class. Hearing that an external heavy was coming in to assess her, Jane had gone to the children and told them that, for once in their lives, they should behave themselves, as Miss X's career was on the line. Children who would walk ten miles to feed a poorly pigeon, but not hesitate to torment a nervous student teacher, had done as she had asked. It seemed a pity that a student, who, with the help of a superordinate external authority in the form of an experienced deputy head, could teach with a modest degree of effectiveness, should be so ineffective on her own. It also confirmed that the ability to control behaviour, in whatever manner, is a 'threshold' measure – if you have enough of it you are over the threshold and can display the rest of your repertoire of professional skills, but too little of it and these may never become apparent.

One of the features of research into classroom behaviour, both in the Leverhulme Primary Project and by others, is that there are many ways of teaching effectively. In the nineteenth century, teacher training institutions were known as 'normal' schools (Wragg 1974). The assumption was that there was some agreed 'norm', some single approved way of teaching that all must copy. It led to Charles Dickens describing M'Choakumchild in *Hard Times* as like 'some one hundred and forty schoolmasters [who] had been turned at the same time at the same factory, on the same principles, like so many pianoforte legs'. The tendency in teacher

training in recent times has been to encourage a variety of approaches to teaching generally and to class management in particular.

Inability to manage classes skilfully is often the single most common reason for failure on teaching practice and for failing the probationary period. Fear of being unable to control a class is often the greatest anxiety of student-teachers before teaching practice (Wragg 1984). The management of people, time and resources is right at the heart of human skill in a variety of occupations, not just teaching. Those who waste resources, fritter away time or alienate their workmates or their customers are often a source of intense irritation. In teaching, the ability to use time skilfully, to win the support of children and to make effective use of what are often scarce resources lies at the heart of professional competence. Time devoted to improving class management is time well spent.

I shall, therefore, adopt the following two principles in what follows:

Class management is what teachers do to ensure that children engage in the task in hand

1 Class management is what teachers do to ensure that children engage in the task in hand, whatever that may be.
2 There are many different ways of achieving the state where children work at the task in hand.

In order to help clarify your own or your colleagues' views of what constitutes effective class management, the following exercise can be undertaken. It is based on, though not identical to, techniques developed in personal construct theory (Kelly 1970), which allows people to examine their own thinking and constructions by comparing and contrasting individuals and concepts.

ACTIVITY 1

Step 1   Think of two teachers who taught you in primary school (or else of two teachers whose teaching you know well). The first teacher (Teacher A) should be someone in whose lessons you felt pupils learned a lot and enjoyed being present. The second teacher (Teacher B) should be a different teacher, one in whose lessons you felt little was learned and which pupils did not seem to enjoy. To refresh your memory, picture Teacher A and Teacher B as clearly as you can in your mind's eye. Without exaggerating, write a brief descriptive paragraph about each in the spaces provided on page 6 or on a separate sheet. These may be quite ordinary things that stick in your mind, such as 'This teacher always had the patience to explain things clearly to you, even if you did not understand first time. I remember feeling really frustrated about a maths problem once, and she just sat and did it with me until I understood the principle'; or, 'This teacher was sometimes unfair in her use of punishments. Once she kept the whole class in at lunchtime just because one boy had knocked someone's gym kit over, and everyone deeply resented it.'

Write your own descriptions in the space provided.

Step 2   Look at your descriptions and assemble a set of dimensions, using adjectives and phrases that are the opposite of each other like 'tidy – untidy' or 'turned up on time – was often late'. It is not essential that Teachers A and B should be the exact opposite of each other on each dimension: for example, they might both have been strict or neither might have been. It is important that you pick out *in your own way* aspects of teaching, especially where class management is involved, and write these down in your own words. For example, your first four pairs might be:

1 Is strict   – Lets children do what they like
2 Has a sense of humour   – Has no sense of humour
3 Is businesslike   – Is slipshod
4 Interested in individuals   – Not interested in individuals

Write up to ten pairs of opposites in the grid below:

1	
2	
3	
4	
5	
6	
7	
8	
9	
10	

TEACHER A

General description

Memorable event 1

Memorable event 2

TEACHER B

General description

Memorable event 1

Memorable event 2

1	Is strict	1 2 ③ 4 5 6 7	Lets children do what they like
2	Has a sense of humour	1 ② 3 4 5 6 7	Has no sense of humour
3	Is businesslike	1 ② 3 4 5 6 7	Is slipshod
4	Interested in individuals	① 2 3 4 5 6 7	Not interested in individuals

Step 3   Now think of 'the ideal teacher', someone who is supreme at working with children. This person might be similar to Teacher A, but not necessarily so, since no one is perfect. You should attempt to define what for you is the ideal teacher on a seven-point scale, using your own list of ten pairs of opposites. For example, suppose you think that your ideal teacher would be slightly strict, have a good sense of humour, be pretty businesslike and be very interested in individuals, then your grid might look like the example above.

Now write your own pairs of opposites in the grid below and rate the ideal teacher by circling the appropriate number on each seven-point scale.

Step 4   The next stage is to think once more about these attributes, but this time to give an honest appraisal of yourself, either as you think you are, if you are already teaching, or as you think you will be when you start. With the thought '*myself*' put a *cross* through the appropriate number on the seven-point scales above. You should do this as honestly as you can, being neither too severe nor too generous with yourself. When you have finished you can compare your self-appraisal with your own ideal. For example, if you saw yourself as fairly permissive, with a bit of a sense of humour, slightly slipshod and interested in individuals, then your grid would look something like the grid on p. 8:

This would show that you are close to what you perceive to be the ideal teacher on two of your dimensions, humour and interest in individuals, but some distance away on strictness and being businesslike. The benefit of this analysis is not that it tells you exactly what kind of person you really are (you would need comments from other people to have a better idea of that), but that it allows you to compare yourself with your ideal on your own set of criteria.

Step 5   There are several possible follow-ups to this exercise.

As an individual you can ask yourself:

- How do I compare with my ideal teacher?
- Will/Should I change on any of these dimensions?

1	1 2 3 4 5 6 7	
2	1 2 3 4 5 6 7	
3	1 2 3 4 5 6 7	
4	1 2 3 4 5 6 7	
5	1 2 3 4 5 6 7	
6	1 2 3 4 5 6 7	
7	1 2 3 4 5 6 7	
8	1 2 3 4 5 6 7	
9	1 2 3 4 5 6 7	
10	1 2 3 4 5 6 7	

1 Is strict	1 2 ③ 4 5 ✗ 7	Lets children do what they like
2 Has a sense of humour	1 ② ✗ 4 5 6 7	Has no sense of humour
3 Is businesslike	1 ② 3 4 ✗ 6 7	Is slipshod
4 Interested in individuals	① ✗ 3 4 5 6 7	Not interested in individuals

A comparison between an 'ideal' (circles) and an actual (crosses) teacher

- Which categories are most worthy of further scrutiny?

In a group you can consider:

- How do group members' views of ideal teachers differ from each other (the circled numbers)?
- What features are in common?
- How different from each other are individual members of the group on their self-ratings (the crossed numbers)?

One approach in a group is for the group leader to synthesize all members' views into a 'master list' of ten pairs of those opposites that appear in various guises in several people's individual lists. Then participants can each rate their own ideal teacher on such a master list and compare the results with those of other members of the group, discussing points of similarity and difference.

Step 6   ACTION   The final stage is to translate analysis into action. First of all, work out what each of your conclusions means in terms of *classroom behaviour*. Reflection on characteristics means little unless you decide what you must *do* to improve practice. Here are two examples of conclusions based on the examples above and how someone might translate these into action.

Conclusion: Need to be a bit more strict

Think about this first. Why do you need to be more strict? If children are misbehaving it may be because the work is boring, unsuitable, over- or under-demanding, rather than because you are too soft.

Possible action includes:

- Deal with misbehaviour as soon as it occurs.
- Make fair use of punishments when appropriate, but also praise good behaviour.
- Clarify classroom rules about movement, talking, setting out of work, etc.
- Make sure task is suitable, clearly defined and children know what they are supposed to be doing.
- Discuss with pupils what sort of misbehaviour is not right, and what steps children should take to be responsible for their own good behaviour.

Conclusion: Need to be more businesslike

If you decide this, then you need to ask yourself why, and also what you understand by 'businesslike'. Do you forget to bring the right materials and books? Are your instructions to the class not clear? Do you not monitor and record children's work effectively?

Possible action includes:

- Prepare lessons more carefully.
- List requirements such as books, materials beforehand and make sure they are available.
- Work out in advance which are the key points you wish to stress when you give instructions or explanations.
- Improve the organization of the beginnings and endings of lessons.
- Look at the layout of the room and how appropriate it is for the activities taking place.

Unit 2

DIFFERENT VIEWS

Given the different temperaments, views, experience and background of primary teachers, it would be astonishing if all responded to the challenge of managing a class in the same way. Though there may, in certain cases, be broad similarities between teachers in the way they handle a disruptive event or organize a project, there will also be significant differences.

ACTIVITY 2

Look at the picture on p. 10. It shows a class of children entering the room in a boisterous manner. During the Leverhulme Primary Project we showed this and other pictures to hundreds of trainee, experienced and supply teachers. Each was asked to comment on the situation with the following story line:

> It is time for the second half of the morning on your first day with this class. They come running back into the room, pushing each other, squealing and laughing. What, if anything, do you do?

Consider and discuss the responses by the four teachers below:

Teacher A

I would wait until they were all in the classroom, then I would use my assertive, cross voice and explain that in my class nobody comes into the classroom behaving like that; that we don't run into any classroom, that we walk into a classroom. And I would send them all outside and make them line up until there was absolute silence and then I would make them walk in, in an orderly manner, and sit down on the chairs properly.

Teacher B

I would send them out into the corridor and then I'd say, 'Your behaviour was disgraceful, disgraceful. Never again shall you enter into my class like that – *my* class by the way – I am your teacher today. Never again enter a class like that. Oh, and by the way, look at my face – I'm not smiling, I'm dead serious.'

Teacher C

If they had come in like that I would have collected them round me, sat them on the floor because they don't look that old and sort of had a talk about why we come in quietly and that I *expect* them to come in and get on with what they're doing quietly.

Teacher D

I'd change the beginning of the lesson and do a 'quietening down' activity. I wouldn't say anything about it at the time, but just before lunchtime I'd say that I didn't like the way they came into the room after break and that I expect them to enter in an orderly manner after lunch.

1 How do they differ?
2 What do you think might be the likely consequences of each response?
3 Which do you most agree and disagree with, and why?

It is interesting to contrast the strategies chosen by the four teachers. Teacher A opts for a firm manner and a 'cross' voice. Ronald King (1978) in his book *All Things Bright and Beautiful?* described various voices commonly used by infant teachers, giving them labels such as, 'Now we are going to do something exciting', 'slightly aggrieved', 'I'm being very patient with you', 'Oh, never mind, don't let's have a fuss', and 'listen to me, I'm saying something

Children burst into room

important'. The use of the voice for emphasis, direction or warning is often a significant feature in class management.

Teacher B, like Teacher A and most of the experienced teachers we interviewed, opted for making the class repeat their entry immediately. However, there is a strong assertion of authority, territory and moral disdain, with phrases like, 'disgraceful, disgraceful', 'never again shall you' and 'my class'. She was a supply teacher, conscious of the need to make her presence felt early, as she met several classes for short periods, hence the phrase, 'I am your teacher today'.

By contrast Teacher C and Teacher D opted for a more low-key approach. Teacher C was firm enough, stressing what she *expected*, but associated herself more closely with the class, sitting on the floor with them, talking through what had happened, using the word 'we' rather than 'you'. There is a noticeable contrast with Teacher B, who puts distance between herself and the children. It is

also different from Teacher D who, in the short term, ignores the unruly entry completely in direct terms, but responds indirectly by changing her lesson plan to introduce a 'quietening down' activity and then by using the next entry as an opportunity to rectify the earlier misdemeanour. Teacher D was a student teacher and her approach illustrates a noticeable difference between students and experienced teachers. Students were more likely in interview to favour the 'talk quietly' or 'change lesson opening' tactic, whereas experienced teachers tended to prefer demanding an immediate re-entry.

SCHOOLS OF THOUGHT

Although teachers have different personal preferences there are certain predominant trends and beliefs that consciously or subconsciously inform and influence their classroom behaviour. This is not to say that teachers occupy permanently one single stereotyped form of management. Though sudden or violent fluctuations of manner are sometimes, in normal circumstances, illustrative of a disturbed personality, in busy classrooms teachers may have to react to several events, each in a quite different tone, within a very short space of time. The fact that the teacher has, for example, reacted in an authoritarian way to someone who has misbehaved, does not mean that every subsequent event should evoke a similar response.

Various standpoints on class management have been endorsed or rejected during the past few years. Below are but seven.

1 Authoritarian

The principal belief here is that teachers are paid to establish and maintain order within a school. They probably, therefore, know best, and should expect to be obeyed. Authoritarianism is sometimes stereotyped as 'hard' or 'unkind', but this need not be the case at all. There are many teachers, who are firmly in charge and give numerous directions, whom one could not describe as lacking kindliness, understanding or concern for the child as an individual. In Victorian times, great stress was laid on the authority of the teacher and classes frequently chanted in unison learned answers to standard questions. Teachers were expected to exercise firm control over behaviour and the knowledge children acquired, and corporal punishment was used extensively. In more recent times, corporal punishment has been abandoned and the role of the teacher has come under close scrutiny, with vigorous debate about whether what is taught should be determined by the class teacher, fashioned by the children themselves or laid down centrally in a national curriculum by statute.

Geoffrey Bantock (1965) asserts what for him is the inescapable 'authority' of the teacher in his book *Freedom and Authority in Education.*

> The Teacher, however much he may attempt to disguise the fact, must, if only because he is not appointed or dismissed by pupils, represent an authority. He must do so, also because he is inescapably 'other' than the children. For one thing, he is older; he has inevitably undergone experiences which give him a different background of assumption from that of his charges. He is, that is to say, psychically different. He has, too, certain legal responsibilities and is answerable to the community at large for aspects of his

behaviour. There is therefore unavoidably, 'mechanically', as it were, a gulf which no attempt at disguise can hide, because it is endemic in the situation, 'given'. Nor do I think that it should be disguised. Power is an inescapable element in adult life, to which we all at some time or other have to come to terms; and I deprecate a great deal of the current insincerity which strives to hide the true situation and thus prepares the child for a fictitious world, not one of reality, even when the circumstance is blanketed under some such grandiose title as 'training in the self-responsibilities of citizenship'. It is to be deprecated for a number of reasons, not least of which is the need to learn respect for the idea of authority as such, as a necessary element in the proper functioning of the community.

Typical classroom behaviour

Teachers would expect to make many of the decisions about content and procedure, with perhaps fewer explanations or justification of the reasons for such decisions. There may be less permitted movement or talking to other pupils. More directions would be given with the intention that they be carried out. Hand raising before speaking would probably be insisted upon.

Comments   Supporters of this mode of management argue that chaos ensues unless a teacher is clearly 'in charge', that children themselves expect teachers to be strict (see page 15), that teachers have the experience to know what children should be doing. Critics argue that authoritarian teaching can easily become repressive, that children need to learn to manage and determine their own behaviour if our rapidly changing society is to be truly democratic.

2 Permissive

This is usually regarded as the polar opposite of authoritarian. Children's freedom to develop autonomy, it is argued, will be inhibited by undue interference from the teacher. The following extract from A.S. Neill's *Summerhill,* illustrated this concept in a form that has been influential in some schools, but rarely copied in its original form.

> Summerhill is a self-governing school, democratic in form. Everything connected with social, or group, life, including punishment for social offences, is settled b⌐

vote at the Saturday night General School Meeting.

Each member of the teaching staff and each child, regardless of his age, has one vote. My vote carries the same weight as that of a seven-year-old.

One may smile and say, 'But your voice has more value, hasn't it?' Well, let's see. Once I got up at a meeting and proposed that no child under sixteen should be allowed to smoke. I argued my case: a drug, poisonous, not a real appetite in children, but mostly an attempt to be grown up. Counter-arguments were thrown across the floor. The vote was taken. I was beaten by a large majority.

The sequel is worth recording. After my defeat, a boy of sixteen proposed that no one under twelve should be allowed to smoke. He carried his motion. However, at the following weekly meeting a boy of twelve proposed the repeal of the new smoking rule, saying, 'We are all sitting in the toilets smoking on the sly just like kids do in a strict school, and I say it is against the whole idea of Summerhill.' His speech was cheered, and that meeting repealed the law. I hope I have made it clear that my voice is not always more powerful than that of a child.

Typical classroom behaviour

Teachers are less likely to issue commands, use reprimands or punishment. Freedom of movement is more likely to be permitted and the buzz of conversation among pupils may be louder. Emphasis will be more on pupils taking responsibility for their own behaviour.

Comments Supporters argue that much of the management in Victorian times was repressive and produced too many uninventive and compliant adults, that children are perfectly capable of sensible behaviour, provided they are trusted. Critics claim that permissiveness too frequently degenerates into a laissez-faire ad-hoc sort of classroom where anything goes and little time is spent on learning, where social chit-chat can consume much of the time in school, at the expense of what the children are supposed to be studying.

a ACTIVITY 3

1 Compare the quotes from Bantock and Neill above.

2 Which parts of each do you agree and disagree with?

3 Are the two viewpoints completely irreconcilable polar opposites of each other?

3 Behaviour modification

This approach is based on the learning theories developed by B.F. Skinner and his associates. We learn best, it is believed, when positive behaviour is *reinforced*, often by reward or recognition. Thus, children who seek attention and are 'told off' are actually being encouraged to misbehave further to attract more attention. The role of the teacher is to help children to learn socially desirable behaviour.

Typical classroom behaviour

Teachers will ignore anti-social behaviour, on the grounds that failure to reinforce it by giving it attention will lead to its extinction, and they reward or publicly recognize approved behaviour, sometimes by giving out tokens, in the belief that this reinforces it and makes it more likely to occur.

Comments This form of management has been criticized, partly because in early work in the United States drugs were used to sedate hyperactive children. Critics argue that the treatment is mechanistic, seeing people as machines not humans, that formal reward systems are merely a form of bribery, and that it is too overt a manipulation of young people. They also say that ignoring misbehaviour does not necessarily improve it and that, in the case of children who use swearwords, for example, 'reinforcement' may come from other pupils. Supporters counter this by saying that most teachers, and indeed most human beings in their relationships generally, use reinforcement techniques, and it is dishonest to pretend otherwise, that many children have learned to behave badly and want to behave well if only someone will show them how, and that 'contract' systems, whereby children specify what they themselves would like to achieve, have removed the 'teacher manipulation' objection.

4 Interpersonal relationships

The belief here is that learning takes place where positive relationships exist between a teacher and class and among pupils. The teacher's role is to develop a healthy classroom climate within which learning will automatically thrive. This approach is often much influenced by the views of Carl Rogers and his followers.

Typical classroom behaviour

Teachers put a premium on personal relationships both between themselves and pupils and among pupils. There may, therefore, be more involvement of pupils in, say, the negotiation of rules, with discussion and suggestion about why these make sense. When problems occur the teacher may employ what Glasser (1969) called 'reality therapy', whereby an interview takes place between the pupil and the teacher with whom he has the strongest rapport to establish why things are going wrong, what are the consequences of the pupil's attitudes and actions, and how he might proceed in future.

Comments Supporters of this point of view regard personal relationships as of crucial importance to all human beings and argue, therefore, that children must learn how to establish positive relationships with their peers and with adults from an early age. They point out how frequently in school, situations that would be difficult in other contexts are easily managed in classrooms where relationships are good. Critics counter that this can easily be overstated, that the pursuit of good relationships can begin to override the acquisition of skills and knowledge, and that there are classrooms where relationships are sound but where little is learned.

5   Scientific

Professor Nate Gage of Stanford University, in his books *The Scientific Basis of the Art of Teaching* and *Hard Gains in the Soft Sciences*, has put forward the proposition that teaching is a science as well as an art, and that teaching can be systematically studied and analysed. Once we know enough, behaviour can be predicted and 'successful' strategies identified. Jacob Kounin, in his book *Discipline and Group Management in Classrooms* used systematic observation of videotapes of primary classroom to identify what he called 'desist' techniques: that is, action by teachers which seemed to be particularly effective when children misbehaved. He did not identify one single 'desist' as supremely effective, but rather described a series of strategies which were used by teachers who appeared to be successful at managing misbehaviour. He gave these strategies somewhat offbeat names like:

withitness   having eyes in the back of your head, thus picking up misbehaviour early.

overlapping   being able to do more than one thing at once: for example, deal with someone misbehaving while at the same time keeping the children you are with occupied.

smoothness   keeping children at work by *not*

(a) intruding suddenly when they are busy (**thrusts**);
(b) starting one activity and then leaving it abruptly to engage in another one (**dangles**);
(c) ending an activity and then coming back to it unexpectedly (**flip-flops**).

overdwelling   skilful teachers avoided staying on an issue for longer than was necessary.

ripple effect   when a teacher interacted with an individual or a small group, 'Haven't you started yet Mary?', 'That's a nice picture, John', the effect rippled outwards to others nearby who 'read' the messages: 'This teacher expects us to have started', 'This teacher is interested in our work' (Fig. 2.1, p. 15).

Typical classroom behaviour

This depends on what classroom research has been brought to teachers' attention, but, in the case of Kounin's successful 'desist' strategies described above, an early years' teacher applying the principle of 'withitness', for example, might, while hearing children read, occasionally glance rapidly round the class to make sure others were engaged in their task. Another teacher might decide to make a quick tour of the classroom immediately the children had begun work, commenting publicly on one or two individuals to exploit the 'ripple effect' and give a message to the whole class about what is expected, what is highly regarded or what is not permitted.

Comments Critics argue that teaching is an art and cannot be analysed or taught in any systematic way, that there is, as yet, not sufficient research evidence to constitute a science of teaching, and that teachers are more influenced by their own personal experience than by what they read in research reports. Supporters point out that medieval doctors defended the use of leeches on similar grounds, that research evidence is necessary if teaching is to move forward, and that rather than replace a teacher's artistry, carefully collected evidence can form what Gage called a 'scientific basis' to enhance it.

6   Social systems

People in school are believed to belong to a sub-system of a wider social organization in which many influences are at work on the group's behaviour. These may be political, social, financial, emotional, etc. Failure to understand these processes, it is said, will inhibit the teacher's ability to work effectively in a school, although learning itself is seen as an individual process.

'Withitness' – the ability to split your attention between the pupils you are with and the rest of the class

Typical classroom behaviour

It is difficult to translate this belief into behavioural terms, but the teacher would probably be interested in the wider aspects of education, be knowledgeable about the school's catchment area, the family background, religious beliefs and community traditions and values.

Comments   Many school problems, argue those interested in this aspect, cannot be dealt with in isolation. Poor housing, financial hardship, family circumstances, parents' employment or lack of it, their education, aspirations and attitudes, all these may exert more powerful influences over pupils' behaviour than anything that happens in school. Teachers need to know about the religious beliefs of the children in their classes, for example, so that they understand why a child might be away from school celebrating a particular festival, or why there might be a particular view of diet, physical education and dance, or family life. Critics counter

by saying that teachers have little or no control over these external factors, and, while able to be sympathetic and understanding, must of necessity act within the framework of the school. Hence the complaint sometimes heard from teachers at conferences, 'I am a teacher, not a social worker'.

7   Folklore

Teachers over the years have built up a stock of 'tricks of the trade'. These can be learned, it is said, and the young teacher will be equipped with an omni-purpose set of recipes, which will be useful in most situations. The most common tips reported by teachers and students interviewed in the Leverhulme Project were: 'Prepare and plan carefully', 'Be well organized and anticipate problems', 'Develop different strategies for different ages of children', 'Establish good personal relationships', 'Be firm in your guidelines, and let children know the limits', 'Keep children busy'.

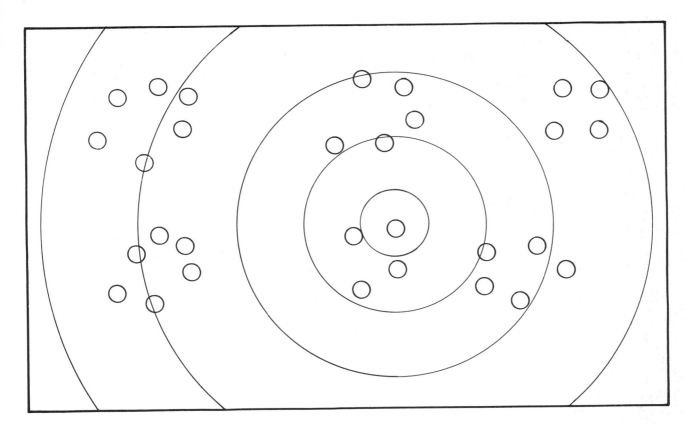

Figure 2.1 'Ripple effect'

Typical classroom behaviour

Once more this depends on the kind of folk-lore which has been purveyed, but someone offered the common tip 'start strictly and ease off later' may well attempt to be more severe than he might otherwise have been in the early stages.

Comments   Those who believe in tips claim that considerable accumulated professional wisdom lies behind them, that such tips are fairly universal in many schools and cultures, and that generations of trainees have gratefully acknowledged their value. Critics say that tips are lacking in any theoretical basis, are random and unrelated to each other, and may suit the person who proffers them but not the recipient.

PUPILS' VIEWS

Kurt Lewin the German social psychologist argued that children of pre-school age were well able to recognize competence in adults (Lewin 1943). Pupils at school have a clear and consistent view of their ideal teacher (Wragg 1984). Surveys over a long

period of time, since the 1930s, show that, in general, they expect teachers to be slightly strict, rather than very strict or permissive. They expect fair use of rewards and punishments, and anyone who needs confirmation of this should simply ask elderly friends and relatives in their 70s or 80s to recall their schooldays. They frequently remember in vivid detail events of their childhood in school, especially where unfairness is involved, for this in particular leaves an abiding impression. Children also prefer teachers whose lessons are interesting, who see them as individuals, who can explain things clearly and who have a sense of humour, but do not engage in sarcasm.

In summary, children tend to prefer teachers who:

- are slightly strict, but not over-severe or permissive
- are fair in their use of rewards and punishments
- treat them as individuals
- are interesting and provide a variety of stimulating work
- are friendly and good humoured, but not sarcastic
- explain things clearly

Child fiddling with pencil case

ACTIVITY 4

Look at the picture showing a child fiddling noisily with his pencil case. The teacher finds that he often does this at the beginning of a lesson. Make a list below of how teachers with different beliefs, influences and practices, as described above, might respond, and then consider what you think would be the consequences of the action or inaction. If you are working with a group of teachers, compare your responses with those of other participants. Decide what this tells you about your own preferences and your likely response to actual classroom behaviour. A sample (but not a model!) response has been entered in the pro-forma on p. 17.

Finally, consider any particular ideas you might try out in your own teaching in future. An example, but one of numerous possibilities, is given below, but you should test out ideas of your own in the

light of your own analysis. Remember the labels 'authoritarian', 'scientific', etc., have sometimes acquired emotive overtones. They are used here for general convenience, and are not meant to be hard-edged stereotypes. Indeed, the notion 'authoritarian' must be dry cleaned of its association with peremptory and insensitive behaviour and it must be recognized that 'scientific' does not imply the precision normally accorded to the hard sciences.

Example ('scientific' category)

The Leverhulme Primary Project found that teachers who took action to deal with misbehaviour early were less likely to have problems than those who allowed it to escalate. If you do not normally take action early, try nipping misbehaviour problems in the bud and then reflect on the outcome.

Teacher response

The teacher decides this is 'attention seeking' and so ignores it, so as not to reinforce it. However, she waits until the boy starts work and then congratulates him for getting going (behaviour modification).

Write more possible responses below

Possible outcomes

It might work as planned and reinforcing positive behaviour might reduce the attention seeking, but it might not be attention seeking in the first place, so the teacher would need to find out why he fiddles with his pencil case (does he not understand what he is supposed to do?)

Write more possible outcomes below

ACTIVITY 5

Step 1   Show the picture on page 10 to pupils in your class or in the age group you normally teach. Ask them the following questions, and then discuss their answers with them. If you are a student or supply teacher make sure that the head and class teacher do not mind your doing this exercise with pupils.

'I want you to think of the best teacher in the whole world. Try to imagine someone who is a brilliant teacher. Now look at this picture. These children rush into the classroom pushing each other out of the way, knocking things over and making a lot of noise. What do you think this brilliant teacher would do if that happened?'

Step 2   Use another picture or make up another storyline and ask children what the imaginary 'perfect teacher' would do.

Step 3   Think about the children's responses to these situations. Do they surprise you? Or are they what you expected? Do they make you think about your own handling of similar situations?

Step 4   (only for the courageous) Ask some children about their views on the 'perfect teacher' and then ask them how they think you are (a) similar and (b) different. (Have a stiff drink ready for afterwards, in case you need it).

FIRST ENCOUNTERS

When people first meet each other in any human social situation a great deal of information is processed very rapidly by those involved. Imagine that you return home one day and switch on the television set to catch up with the news. As the picture comes into focus the screen is filled by someone being interviewed. In an exceedingly short time you would have probably (though not always) formed conclusions about the interviewee's approximate age, regional or other accent, intelligence, sex, social group, likely political views, education, and you would have sifted and analysed a great deal of other information. Your inferences may be accurate (that the man is in his fifties, or that the woman is Scottish), but they may also be inaccurate. For example, you may wrongly suppose that someone with a 'posh' accent is 'stuck up' or that the person in an open-necked shirt is casual, when it may in fact be a distinguished judge being interviewed in his garden on a Sunday afternoon. There is in social psychology a phenomenon known as 'assortative mating', that is, the tendency of people to marry someone of similar intelligence, personality or social background. Yet few adults wander around social events or discos with WISC intelligence tests or Cattell Personality Questionnaires in their back pockets. What they do is scan fellow human beings with great rapidity on a comprehensive and often subconscious checklist.

When teachers meet children for the first time a similar process of mutual appraisal takes place. Although most teachers and children are fresh to each other in September, the reputation of either group may have preceded it – the known 'martinet' who stands no nonsense, the 'difficult' class or pupil. Most schools make a special scene-setting effort at the beginning of the year. Studies of secondary teachers' first encounters (Wragg 1984) showed that teachers often tried to make a big and sometimes macho impact in their very first lesson. By contrast, when we studied primary classrooms in the

Leverhulme Project during the first few days of the school year, though there was some emphasis on being in charge, the main stress, especially with classes of young infant pupils, was on friendliness and creating an atmosphere of welcome. In this unit there will be a number of references to the Leverhulme Study (conducted at Exeter University), which observed and interviewed experienced teachers, supply teachers and student teachers in relation to their first meetings with a new class.

Many schools invest time and energy at the beginning of the school year to establish a climate which, they hope, will last through the year. There may be mention in the first assembly of the need for high achievement, good behaviour, tidiness, thought for others, or whatever the school wishes to stress. Individual teachers will then immediately reinforce, or occasionally confound, these aspirations in their own classrooms. In interview before the start of the school year, experienced heads and teachers are usually very clear about what they will do at the beginning of the school year. There are two groups of teachers, however, who do not have the same advantages as full-time class teachers. These are supply teachers and students on school experience or teaching practice. Supply teachers often have considerable teaching experience and clarity in their own minds about such matters as classroom rules, but have to manage numerous first encounters at various stages of the school year, without the benefit of the collective effort made by others in early September. Student teachers suffer a double disadvantage. They, too, arrive part way through the school year, and therefore miss the support of the whole school's initial effort of the previous September, but in addition they are often unsure about what should be their own rules and what sort of relationships they will seek to establish.

First meetings with classes go through a predictable series of stages, albeit with considerable

expectati-

individual variations according to the school's and teacher's preferred style, the age, nature and size of the class, and certain unpredictable events. The sequence is made up of six key phases of varying length, intensity and importance:

> Preparation and planning – entry into school building – entry into classroom or home base – teacher's opening words – first 'lesson' – rest of first day.

1   Preparation and planning

In some cases teachers are able to meet their 'new' class at the end of the previous school year, either as a group or individually. This is not always possible, however, and in any case the first sustained encounter is likely to occur when the teacher or student takes over the class on a more permanent basis. Consider these two teachers talking about their preparation for their first day with a class:

Teacher A (reception class teacher):

I try to give a lot of thought to the layout of my room. I got a shock when I started my first job. I suddenly thought, 'I've never had to set out a room before.' On teaching practice you always took over from what the class teacher had set up. With reception class children you've got such a mixture. Some look quite cocky, whereas others are very pale and a bit frightened about starting school. I like to lay the tables out with plenty for them to do, so I put things like jigsaws, construction toys, building blocks, picture books, that sort of thing, on each table. When they first come in we all sit on the carpet and I ask them their names and if they know anybody else in my class or in another class. When they've all arrived and we've had a little talk I put them at tables so they can get on with an activity straightaway and feel more at home.

Teacher B (supply teacher):

Basically if I'm approaching a new class, I'm getting myself ready to get in there fairly early – I'm usually in a half hour, forty minutes, before I actually meet a class, because you want to put over the idea that you're well organized and a together person. I think the worst thing a supply can do is to be dithery in front of a new class. It's important that you are competent and confident with taking a register and

you know how the dinner money is slotted in and things like this, even if you are thinking, 'Well, they don't do their dinner money like so and so; this is totally wrong or something.' You've got to get a bit of street credibility fairly early on I think.

ACTIVITY 6

1   Compare the two statements by Teacher A and Teacher B.

2   What control does each have over such matters as room layout, emotional tone, curriculum-related activities, discipline?

3   What are the general differences between experienced teachers starting with a new class in September and supply teachers or student teachers meeting a new class in mid-year?

2   Entry into building

This is where whole school policy can be important. Some schools have a phased start, especially for reception class children, who may come in one or two at a time so they can be welcomed and accompanied to their new class, others have a single mass entry at a given time on the first morning of the school year. In one school we observed, such was the chaos of the entry that individual teachers were struggling to establish order in the first few minutes of their first session with their new class. In many schools, children are escorted in carefully by the head and staff and there is a well-defined procedure for commencing the school year, either with a set of reception routines or with an assembly.

The first school assembly in schools is often one in which there is some kind of exhortation. It may be direct or indirect, by instruction or through a story. Among themes, statements and events, in addition to the hymns and prayers, recorded in twenty schools by observers studying the first week of the school year in the Leverhulme Project were the following, which illustrate a range of purposes: control, inspiration, informing, laying down of rules, outlining of expectations, establishment or reinforcement of school ethos, assertion of community value:

* The head praised pupils on how smart they looked and asked them to keep it up.

- 'When you come into assembly, imagine a zip across your mouth. It is your responsibility to keep it closed.'
- Class seven (the oldest pupils) had had a poor reputation the year before. The head told them they would be expected to behave well and show a high degree of responsibility now they were the top class.
- A theme 'the importance of friendship' was introduced.
- The children were told the story of Robert the Bruce and the moral message it contained, to keep on trying, was emphasized.
- The head said that the school rules were based on 'common sense, such as taking care of people'.
- Children were told not to come to school before 9 o'clock as they would not be allowed into the building.
- The head asked pupils to look at her during assembly when she was talking. One small group of pupils did not do this, so she stared at them until they did.

3 Entry into classroom

In the Leverhulme Project most observers reported a high level of excitement during the first few minutes of the new school year. Primary children returning to school after six weeks or so are eager to find out who is in their class, what their friends did on holiday, who is sitting where. There was often a rush for seats, or else children stood talking by the door uncertain what was happening. Some teachers insisted in an orderly line-up outside the classroom, talked to the children in the corridor or whatever space the queue occupied, accompanied them into the room, assigned places and moved on to the next phase.

a ACTIVITY 7

Step 1 Read the following report of the first morning at school in a class of 5-year-olds, many of whom were starting school for the first time.

> The school is a large nursery and first school for 3- to 8-year-olds in the middle of a huge working-class estate. From 8.30 onwards children arrive, some alone, some in twos and threes, sometimes with, sometimes without their parents. Whole families appear, mother, grandma, grandad, the child starting school, often a younger brother or sister, maybe two, with one in a pushchair, even the

> family dog. It is a big family occasion. By 9 o'clock most children are in school and the street outside is deserted apart from the occasional passer-by or late arrival.

> Mrs A has about two-thirds of her class present. She sits in a chair with the children around her feet. They talk about dinners, classroom rituals, who knows whom in the class and where children might sit. Every five minutes or so a parent appears at the door with a child. An extra teacher, brought in for the first week, is on hand to feed in the latecomers. By 9.30 the class appears to be complete and children are assigned to tables where they choose an activity from several possibilities. At 10.20 there is an ear-splitting yell from down the corridor. The last arrival has appeared. She is clearly not enamoured of the idea of coming to school and her cries of 'No, mummy, I don't want to go', are joined in counterpoint by her mother's audible threats, bribes and oaths, 'I'll come and fetch you at tea time', 'You've *got* to go to school or I'll get into trouble.' Outside Mrs A's classroom the extra supply teacher attempts to soothe parent and child. 'What's her name? Tina is it? Well, come with me, Tina, and I'll take you into Mrs A's room.' Tina kicks her violently on the shin.

Step 2 Imagine you are Mrs A, a less painful role than that of the supply teacher. What would you do as Tina is brought into your classroom? If you are working in a group, discuss your suggestions with others. Consider the likely outcomes of your strategies. What appears to be the nature and rationale of each of the possibilities? Containment? Welcome? Threat? If you teach older pupils discuss the problem of an older child who clearly appears to have problems settling into a new class. How would you explore the possible reasons for such unhappiness? What steps would you take in various circumstances (e.g. if the child were without friends, unable to understand the work, unsettled at home).

Step 3 Consider and discuss the outcome of Tina's arrival at school, as described by the observer:

> The supply teacher brings Tina and her mother into the classroom. She sits Tina down at a table and starts to do a jigsaw with her. 'I'm just going to have a word with Mrs A, I'll be back in a second.' Meanwhile, Tina's mother slips gratefully out of the room. A brief ten second conversation between the supply teacher and Mrs A follows, in which

the supply teacher says she will leave Tina to get on with the jigsaw. She returns to the table and crouches alongside Tina, 'Oh well done, you're good at jigsaws, aren't you, Tina?' With that she mutters a vague, 'I'll be back soon' and leaves the room. A couple of minutes later Mrs A goes over to Tina, 'You've nearly finished that Tina, well done. Here's a box of building bricks. When you've finished see if you can build something nice and then I'll come and have a look at it.'

For the whole of the day Tina worked assiduously alongside the rest of the class, slightly reserved, but indistinguishable from the others, doing the activities, eating her lunch, playing in the playground during breaks. The supply teacher made a brief return visit to see how she was, but by then she was immersed in constructing an elaborate arrangement of building bricks and barely looked up. At 3.15 she listened attentively as the teacher read the class a story, congratulated the children on their good behaviour and said she was looking forward to seeing them all the following day.

At 3.30 the bell rang for the end of school and parents clustered outside the classroom to collect their children. Tina's mother appeared, pale faced and anxiously asking how she had got on. 'Fine', replied Mrs A, 'see you tomorrow Tina', whereupon Tina burst into tears. Her mother may well have been convinced that she had spent the day on the rack. The following day, however, Tina came to school on time, was calm in appearance and never again manifested outward signs of distress about school.

4   Teacher's opening words

Fewer teachers than one would have expected greeted the class at the beginning of the first lesson. Most frequently teachers sought to gain attention with some kind of central presence and a 'public voice' statement. A wide range of opening statements was recorded, including the following:

'Good morning everyone, did you have a good holiday?'

'Is everyone happy with where they're sitting? I want to introduce a new boy who's just joined us in school.'

'Right. I'm letting you sit where you want for the time being, so don't fuss, settle down.'

'Could you all please listen now? Now, let's have a look at your haircuts! What's new?'

'Where shall I sit? (standing with stool in hand) I usually sit in this corner.'

This shows something of a range of purposes and strategies for obtaining attention, depending on the context. If children settled quickly, a friendly opening, setting a relaxed social climate, was frequently used. If they milled around in confusion, a much more staccato response resulted, often incorporating an order or command, like the teacher who shouted, as children bunched by the door, chattering noisily, 'Don't worry about pegs and bags, go into the classroom quietly and stand behind a chair, any chair.' Attention was usually sought to take a register, but seating, allocation of coat pegs or social chat also featured.

Pupil responses were also varied. In most cases there was a positive response and the children fell quiet or obeyed instructions. In a few cases where they did not, teachers usually reacted immediately, sometimes by simply calling out the name of the misbehaving pupil(s), sometimes by standing with hands on hips until there was silence, occasionally with mild sarcasm ('I hope you at the back heard what I said').

5 The first 'lesson'

One significant difference is often detected between student and experienced teachers in the context of first encounters. Students tend to concentrate most on the subject content or topic of first lesson activities, whereas experienced teachers spend more time and effort establishing a climate, assigning seating, usually on a free or 'moderated' choice basis, with the teacher exercising the occasional right of veto, giving out new pencils and books, explaining facilities in the room, and the eventual

activity seems to be of secondary importance at this initial stage. Within half an hour, however, most classes were working at some prescribed assignment ('what I did on holiday' still being a firm fixture) or being asked to choose a book from the library or the reading corner, while the teacher dealt with administrative matters or with pupils who had questions or problems.

6 The rest of the first day

The first day of school serves a wide variety of purposes. There are inescapable classroom rituals, like seating, dinner money and registration to be dealt with; in addition, teachers are conscious of the need to lay down rules of conduct (see Unit 4), establish a working and social climate, signal what level of noise they will tolerate, deal with personal problems, children new to the school, uncertainties and queries from parents. Whereas teachers of older pupils can often take for granted that children will know the school's routines and expectations, though they may need reminding of them, teachers of reception class or first year juniors have to induct new classes into the school for the very first time, with all the sociological complexities that implies. Student and supply teachers are spared that side of induction, but have to read numerous messages, risk confusing children by introducing roles or routines at variance with what they are used to, or, indeed, themselves being confused wittingly or unwittingly by children's accounts of what is normally expected.

 ACTIVITY 8

Imagine you are taking a class for the first time, or, if you are about to take a real new class, address the questions below with the actual class in mind.

1 What would you like to know about the class *in advance*, and why?

2 What sort of topic or theme will you choose for this first lesson and why?

3 What will you be doing and thinking about:
   (a) an hour before the lesson?
   (b) five minutes before the lesson?

4 Do you plan to be present before the class arrives, if this is possible? If not, why not?

5 If you are present outside the room or home base before the session begins what will you be doing:
(a) before entering the room?
(b) as the children enter the room?

6 How will you begin the lesson:
(a) if the class settles down quickly?
(b) if the class is slow to settle?

7 How do you think the class will see you on first meeting you?

8 Are there any rules you will want to establish from the beginning? (and why are these your most pressing rules?)

9 What kind of relationship would you like to have with the class in the longer term, and how will you set about establishing it?

10 What teaching strategies, so far as you can see, will you employ during the first session – groupwork? individual assignments? whole class teaching? question and answer? writing? reading? giving instructions?

a ACTIVITY 9

If you are taking a new class, analyse your actual first session with them in the light of your plans in Activity 8.

A *Preparation and planning*

How effective was your preparation? Was there information you would have liked about the children but did not get?

B *Lesson beginning*

Were you present when the class arrived? What happened? How did they enter the room? How did you introduce yourself? Did the class settle quickly?

C *First impression*

What do you think was the class's first impression of you? Circle a point on the scales below:

brisk, businesslike	1 2 3 4 5 6 7	slipshod
warm, friendly	1 2 3 4 5 6 7	aloof
stimulating	1 2 3 4 5 6 7	dull
well prepared	1 2 3 4 5 6 7	badly prepared
strict	1 2 3 4 5 6 7	permissive

Is this what you would like in the longer term? If not, what can you do to change children's perceptions of you? What do you think children told their parents about their new teacher when they got home?

D *Rules*

What school and classroom rules emerged, either because you stated them or because you reacted to some event?

E *Content*

You may not have been able to spend much time on your actual topic or lesson content in your first session, but how did children react to their first task? Were they busy? bored? confused? intrigued? indifferent? How did the session end?

F *Names*

Think of the class concerned and write below the names of any pupils to whom you can put a face.

G *Follow-up action*

Ask yourself the following:

1 Are your rules the same as other teachers'? How do children know what is and what is not permitted?

2 To what extent does your first session reflect the kind of relationship you would like with the class in the longer term? What should you do in future lessons to establish the sort of relationships you wish to have?

3 Look at your answers to F above. Which children's names do you know and why these? Did they misbehave? Have you taught them before? See if you can learn all the children's names soon. Consider those whose names come less easily to mind and see if you can get to know them better. Who are they? Are they new? or just quiet and well behaved?

First lesson and first day endings

Just as first encounters have an opening, so they have a conclusion, and lesson and day endings can be just as important as beginnings, for closure is something that will happen every day of the year. In most of the first encounters we observed, the ending of the first session and the first day were slightly formal. About half the classes were asked to line up, in most cases because the day was to end with a school assembly to which they were to walk in an orderly fashion. In the rest, children were mainly asked to leave in groups, sometimes one table at a time, occasionally the 'quietest' table first, once or twice in pairs. Usually children had to clear away first and put away their chairs, either beneath or on top of the table. Few teachers gave warning of the end of the session or day, though one or two would announce that in five or ten minutes there would be an assembly, or school would finish, so children should begin to tidy away or complete what they were doing. With young children the day was sometimes concluded with a story or a talking session, where children were seated on a mat at the teacher's feet and the day was reviewed or the next day was discussed.

Children's personal needs

There are several issues that are quite important for children but may be overlooked by teachers. For new pupils especially there may be some anxiety about the conventions in their new school and how quickly they can learn these. It may concern something simple like cleanliness or toilet conventions. What do you do, pupils will want to know, if you want to wash your hands or go to the toilet? Can you just go? Must you ask the teacher? A host of other minor matters may also be in children's minds: Where do you hang your coat? Is it in order to have your bag on the table? the floor? What happens at registration? assembly? dinner time? playtime? How should work be set out? These issues will also be addressed in Unit 4.

 ACTIVITY 10

1 Make a list of matters to do with classroom routines and personal needs which you may need to consider.

2 How will you communicate with children what they should do or what you expect or permit?

3 Are any of these matters a special problem? If so, what can you do about it?

THE TWO Rs – RULES AND RELATIONSHIPS

Many human activities are governed by rules, some explicit and often available in written form, others implicit, unwritten, unspoken even. If we were to try to play a game like chess without observing the rules it would either consist of constant negotiation, or it would be chaotic, or it would collapse under a welter of argument. On the other hand, few families have a written set of rules about mealtimes, television watching or use of the bathroom. Such codes as govern these family matters have often been worked out by trial and error, by sustained informal negotiation over a long period of time.

RULES

Rules in school are of several kinds. There are *national rules*, many incorporated in Acts of Parliament, which govern such matters as pupil attendance, parental rights, use of punishments; there are *local authority rules*, perhaps a code of laboratory safety or what teachers must do on field trips; there are also *school rules* which may be similar to or different from those of other schools, and these can concern dress, behaviour in the playground or use of facilities. Finally, there are *teachers' rules* on matters such as talking, movement, the setting-out of work or disruptive behaviour.

The question of rules is closely bound up with, but also distinct from, that of relationships. The relationship between two or more people is to some extent affected by the rule conventions under which it operates. As Bantock (1965) said in the quotation on page 11, teachers are paid to be present and are therefore different from pupils. They also have legal and contractual obligations, to act as a parent, in *loco parentis*, which means that, to some extent, their relationship with children is affected by what a court might require of them. Should there be an

accident, teachers can avoid legal action for negligence by acting as a responsible parent would, summoning help, checking that the child is in good hands, communicating with those who need to know. When sour relationships develop, it is sometimes because rules are perceived to be unfairly or inconsistently applied, or because there is dissent or uncertainty about the rules themselves.

An American investigator (Buckley 1977) conducted a case study of a primary classroom to see what rules emerged. Out of thirty-two rules eventually compiled, some fifteen emanated from outside the classroom, usually from the head. Within the first six days of the school year, twenty-two of the thirty-two had been spoken of in some form or another by the teacher. However, although some rules were stated explicitly early in the school year, it was common for others to emerge by case law. On one occasion in the third week of term, a pupil played in a certain courtyard area of the school during break and was told by the teacher on duty that this was not allowed, yet no formal announcement had ever been made. Given the many rules and conventions governing behaviour in primary schools, it was hardly surprising that the teacher in Buckley's study did not read out all thirty-two rules plus accompanying conventions on the first morning – it would have been too much to recall and would have suggested that school is solely about rules. Some rules noted in the study were even expressed through euphemism. When the teacher expressed dismay about someone who 'had big eyes', this was not a slur on Mickey Mouse, but rather a coded message that a pupil had been spotted looking at a neighbour's paper during a test.

Take as an example the common rule, 'Don't call out, put your hand up if you want to speak'. I have

ACTIVITY 11

1 Write down the three or four most important rules you can think of for your own classroom.
   (i)

   (ii)

   (iii)

   (iv)

2 Write down some other, less important rules that occur to you.
   (i)

   (ii)

   (iii)

   (iv)

3 Discuss the following:
   (i) How would you classify each of your rules? (movement? property? relationships? school work?)

   (ii) Why is your first set of rules more important than your second set?

   (iii) Take one or two of your more important rules and describe how you established them (in written form? did you tell people what you expected? did you wait until the rule was broken and then react?)

   (iv) What do you do when someone breaks each of your rules?

   (v) How do your rules reflect on and affect your relationships with pupils?

observed several different ways of establishing this, including the following:

✳ _____

Teacher A   'One thing I want everybody to be clear about in my class is that you must put your hand up whenever you want to say something. I don't want anyone calling out. If everyone calls out then we can't hear what anybody is saying.'
(Early in the first lesson of the year).

Teacher B   'What do we always do before we want to speak?'
(An odd one this. It happened early on the first day of school, and although teachers sometimes use 'we' when they mean 'you', it seemed especially strange in this context since she never raised her own hand. Moreover, when a pupil called out, 'Put your hand up', she replied, 'that's quite right, Alison', even though Alison had, herself, called out – a mixed set of messages).

Teacher C   'I'm getting a bit concerned about everybody just calling out "Miss, Miss" all the time. Let's see you put your hands up and then I'll decide who speaks.'
(On the second day, when the class had become noisy).

There are certain differences as well as similarities here. All three teachers were seeking to achieve the same goal, that of persuading children to raise their hands before speaking, but whereas Teacher A stated this explicitly as a rule clearly on the first day, Teacher C waited until some degree of disorder occurred. Teacher A also gave an explanation, self-evident maybe, of why the rule existed. When we interviewed teachers about classroom rules during the Leverhulme Project these same differences in taste and practice emerged. One teacher said she devoted the first session of the year largely to classroom rules, while another said that there was little point in laying down rules at the beginning as 'they wouldn't remember them anyway'. The majority of teachers, about three-quarters, however, said that they would expect to introduce rules during the first day and subsequently whenever the need arose.

Interviews with teachers showed that rules fell under certain clear headings. These included the following, with some specific examples in each case.

Movement

Walk quietly.
No running.
Ask first if you want to go to the toilet.
Don't just wander around the room, unless you're getting something.

Talking

Don't talk when I'm talking to you.
You should only be talking to each other if it's about your work.
Don't talk when someone is answering a question.
Only one person talking at a time.
No shouting out.
Put your hands up, if you want to ask a question.
Silence during registration.
Silence in the library area.

Work-related

Being able to work independently on your own.
Being able to work harmoniously in a group.
Working quietly even if the teacher is out of the room.
Getting out your own tray at the beginning of the day, after lunch or after playtime and then starting work without having to be told.
Not distracting or spoiling the concentration of others when they are working.

Presentation

Knowing how to set out work and when to hand it in.
Taking care with content.

Safety

Care with cupboards, sinks.
Care with scissors, rulers, pencils.
No swinging on chairs.
No playing on slippery banks in wet weather.

Space

Not allowed in classroom at break.
During wet weather being allowed inside school or classroom to read, play games or sit quietly.
'This classroom is a work area, not a play area.'

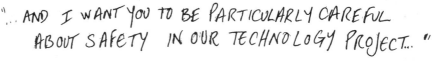

Materials

Equipment to be handled carefully and kept in proper place.
Keep library books tidy.
Know the correct place for returning equipment or unused materials.
Put things away properly at the end of the day.
Clothing and PE equipment to be kept on pegs.
No writing on desks or book covers.
Return borrowed items to their owner.
Stack chairs on or under tables or desks at the end of the day.

Social behaviour

Show consideration for others.
Be willing to share things and co-operate.
'Don't go into someone else's tray unless you've been told to.'
Be polite and thoughtful, treat others as you would like to be treated yourself.
Show good manners.

Clothing

Clothing to be neat and clean.
Wear uniform properly (i.e. school tie).
All clothing to be labelled.
During hot weather sleeves may be rolled up, cardigans, jackets, pullovers and ties removed.

ACTIVITY 12

1   Consider the sets of rules above. Which do you find most important and which seem more trivial? Which would you wish to see in operation in your own classroom, and which not?

2   Take some particular rules, perhaps 'Don't go into someone else's tray unless you've been told to', 'consideration for others', or 'being able to work independently on your own' and discuss how a teacher might (a) establish (b) explain the need for and (c) fine tune such a rule.

3   Choose some rules about which different teachers in the same school might disagree:

(a) what problems might occur (b) what solutions might be found to avoid difficulties. Such rules as 'not being allowed in classroom at break time', 'working quietly even if the teacher is out of the room' and 'knowing how to set out work and when to hand it in' are worth considering here.

4   Discuss the extent to which there should be uniformity and what degree of diversity is permissible in different teachers' classroom rules and conventions within the same school.

NEGOTIATION AND CIRCLE TIME

Relatively few teachers negotiate rules with pupils and, certainly in most of the lessons I have observed, the teacher has either announced, defined or clarified the main rules. Yet there is a view held by writers such as Glasser (*Schools without Failure*, 1969) and Gordon (see Duke 1979) that class management problems are made easier if children can understand why certain rules apply, or are consulted about the sort of behaviour that is desirable in a classroom. Glasser argued that it was worth teachers spending some time explaining what rules they believed in, but also asking pupils to suggest adjustments or new rules of their own. Gordon proposed that teachers could discuss rule-related problems to see who 'owns' it, whether it was the teacher, the pupil, or a shared responsibility. It is well worth creating the time for discussion of what is happening in the classroom, and 'Circle Time', as it is sometimes called, when pupils sit round and discuss the process of teaching and learning with their teacher, can be a valuable lubricant, though it should never become an over-indulgence.

I once observed a secondary science teacher during the first laboratory-based session with a new class of first year pupils. Most of his colleagues simply gave out the local authority's rules on laboratory safety and told pupils to observe them, but he began by saying, 'A laboratory can be a dangerous place and so I want you to make up and write down some rules which will help us avoid having accidents.' Most of the LEA rules like 'no running or pushing', 'handle equipment carefully', 'be careful with flames or acids', were anticipated by the class, so that when he gave out copies of the actual rules they were pleased at their success. Matters like 'wearing goggles', which no-one had suggested, were then discussed.

There is a very important fundamental question about negotiation which must always be addressed: that is, what is or should be negotiable at all. Clearly, matters such as safety on a field trip in potentially dangerous terrain are definitely not open to negotiation. Teachers may help children to understand the need for wearing proper clothing, staying away from dangerous places and not taking risks, but there is absolutely no question of teachers' legal responsibilities being negotiated away. On the other hand, encouraging children to face up to matters such as self-discipline, or respect for others, is something that happens in families and can take place in schools, depending on the age, understanding and background of the children concerned. Teachers in the end must take responsibility for rules, even if they endorse sensible proposals from children.

There are several ways, therefore, in which rules can be introduced. In summary these include, with examples:

General explanation   'I want to see you showing consideration for other children.'

Specific prescription   'In my class you must put your hand up when you want to say something.'

Rule with explanation   'I don't want anyone pushing and shoving near that sink, because someone's going to spill water on the floor and slippery floors cause accidents.'

General question   'How can we make sure no-one gets hurt when we're doing P.E.?'

Specific question   'What would happen if nobody in the school had name tags on their clothes?'

Case law   'All the children in the home corner come out here. Now why do you think I've asked you to come out?' 'Because we're shouting'. 'That's right, now please go back and work quietly.'

Negotiation   'I've allowed you to talk to each other while you're doing your projects, but it's getting far too noisy, so let's just discuss for a minute what we can do about it.'

a ACTIVITY 13   CIRCLE TIME

This activity should be completed at the beginning of the year, but it can be done later, especially if a class is not behaving in an orderly manner. Some teachers prefer children to be seated in a circle for it, but this is not essential. Students or inexperienced teachers should only do this in close collaboration with someone more experienced. The form and wording will need to be modified according to the age, ability and background of the pupils.

1 Explain to the class that, as you will be working together in future, you all need to be clear about behaviour.
2 Ask orally, or in writing, for 'Reasons why we come to school', and then discuss these. Most children will give replies like 'To learn to read and write' or 'To help us get a job', but other answers like 'Because we have to' are worth discussing.
3 Ask children to suggest or write down some simple rules of behaviour which will help everyone learn better. This will often produce suggestions like 'Don't interfere with others who are working', or 'Don't mess about'. Related matters can then be raised, like 'What about safety?' (no running, no pushing), 'What about when we're discussing something?' (no calling out, listen to others) or 'What about when we're working in groups?' (share things, wait your turn, don't do down others).
4 Decide which are the important rules, and, if this is done part way through the year, identify those rules that are most often broken.
5 Get everyone to make a special effort to establish a climate that helps children learn and work harmoniously together.

RELATIONSHIPS

Much of what has been covered in this Unit is not just a matter of rules but also of personal relationships. A good example of the way in which rules and relationships can overlap is over the matter of consistency. If teachers are inconsistent then considerable irritation can ensue. The following observation in a class of 8–9-year-olds illustrates this point well.

The teacher is working at the desk and the pupils too are supposed to be getting on quietly with their work. When children want help, some put up their hand and wait for the teacher to look up, others go over to her desk. Eventually, when one child moves out of her seat to approach the teacher, she intervenes: 'Don't come out to my desk. If you want help, put your hand up and I'll come to you. Now go and sit down and put your hand up.' The girl sits down and raises her hand. After a few seconds the teacher goes over to discuss her questions and then returns to her desk. Subsequently another pupil is told not to interrupt the teacher, but some children

still approach the desk and are given help. One girl sits with her hand raised for over five minutes. It is not until she calls out 'Miss' that the teacher goes over.

In another situation, where children had been asked not to leave their seats, a teacher of 7–8-year-olds was much more consistent and also more attentive. When three children came up to her she said, 'Now why are there one, two, three people here?' One sat down and put his hand up. The teacher walked past the other two and dealt with this query. The other two sat down and raised a hand, so she went to each of them too.

Personal relationships between teacher and pupils can be shaped in many locations and contexts. Consider just some of these, both positive and negative in effect.

Academic	Explaining patiently to pupil who does not understand new concept. Making sarcastic remark to someone who doesn't understand new concept.
Managerial	Smiling at and thanking someone who has helped clear away. Blaming someone for mess, choosing wrong pupil.
Social	Chatting to children as they enter classroom about what they did at the weekend. Belittling someone's hobby or family/cultural interest.
Expectation	Looking for positive qualities and achievements in children. Having low expectations or always focusing on the negative side of pupils' work or behaviour.
Home/school/ community	Talking positively with parents and members of children's communities. Showing no interest in children's origins and values.
Individual	Taking a personal interest in children as individuals. Seeing class entirely as a group without individual identities.

Personal relationships between pupil and pupil are just as important as those between teacher and pupil. Teachers can play a significant part in the establishment of such relationships. During the Leverhulme Project one of the research techniques used was to identify events that happen in classrooms and that seem to be indicative of the styles, preferences and effects of various teachers.

The long wait for attention

Several hundred such critical events were collected and analysed. In each case the observer records what led up to the event, what happened and what appeared to be the outcome. After the lesson the teacher, and sometimes the pupils, were interviewed to elicit their view of what had happened. One of the aspects of teaching highlighted in this way was what teachers did about relationships between pupils. Consider the following two accounts, in the first of which the teacher took positive action and in the second of which the teacher barely intervened.

Event 1 – Teacher intervenes

The teacher was talking to a class of 11-year-olds about Europe. She asked the class to give her the names of as many European countries as they could think of and then wrote them on the board prior to developing the theme further. At one point a boy had a whispered conversation with another sitting nearby and then put up his hand. When called upon

he answered, 'France'. The teacher praised him fulsomely, 'Well done, Stefan, good boy.'

Teacher's comment

Stefan is a new boy who has just moved to England from abroad. He doesn't speak much English, so we've had a chat about what we can all do to help him. Michael was looking at the map with him and telling him the English names of countries.

Event 2 – Little intervention

A class of 8–9-year-olds was working in groups on their set task. Three girls were sitting together at the same table. From time to time two of the girls, Alice and Rachel, would behave in an unpleasant manner towards the third, Caroline, refusing to lend her a rubber, throwing things at her, preventing her from working. The teacher goes over to the trio and speaks to Caroline: 'Just ignore them, Caroline, and get on with your work.' From time to time she looks at Alice's and Rachel's work, but does not refer to their behaviour.

Teacher's comment

Alice and Rachel are just attention-seekers. Alice in particular is a very unsettled child. She does the same thing in the playground, picks an argument with somebody and runs up to whoever is on duty shouting about the offence being committed against her, when in fact she's started it herself, or telling tales about somebody else doing something to somebody. It's a lot of attention-seeking behaviour.

This second event in particular raises important issues. To some extent, by ignoring what she rightly or wrongly judges to be attention-seeking, the teacher is following the tenets of behaviour modification. According to these, 'bad' behaviour should be ignored so that it is extinguished through not being reinforced. However, the corollary to this is that 'good' or approved behaviour should be reinforced. Unless Alice and Rachel are recognized by the teacher when their behaviour is positive, then, according to the behaviourist view, no reinforcement will take place and the process will be random. Critics of behaviourism, on the other hand, would argue that improving personal relationships between pupils, or between teacher and pupils, is not just a matter of addressing symptoms, but much more fundamental. Thus, in this situation, they would argue, it is not sufficient merely to 'extinguish' anti-social behaviour, the teacher should rather try to find out why Alice seeks attention and probably discuss with her the effects of this behaviour on others.

1 Find a fellow teacher or student who is willing to be observed. It is a useful paired activity, whereby two students, or teachers, or a teacher and a student, can observe each other's lessons.
2 During the lesson, look for something that happens that illustrates relationships between (a) teacher and pupil(s) and (b) pupil(s) and pupil(s). The events do not have to be spectacular: indeed, in most cases they will be ordinary everyday happenings, including, perhaps, a few words, a smile, a telling-off, some movement or some humour.
3 Fill in a pro-forma like the one on page 34.
4 After the lesson, interview the teacher about the event, using a neutral opening like, 'Towards the beginning of the lesson you spoke to Caroline about something that had just happened at her table. Can you tell me a bit about what happened?' You can then probe further with 'Why' questions or 'What do you think the effect was?' Avoid starting off with leading or tendentious questions such as, 'Why on earth did (or didn't) you . . .?' or 'Why were you so soft on Rachel and Alice . . .?'
5 Interview pupils only if the teacher concerned and the head of the school agree. Interviewing pupils about their classroom relationships with each other and/or their teacher is a sensitive matter, which must be handled in a thoroughly professional way. Student or inexperienced teachers should certainly ensure that they receive proper supervision for such an exercise.
6 See what generalizations and what specific points emerge from your classroom scrutiny. For example, it might seem, as a general conclusion, that the teacher has good relationships with the girls in the class, but less happy ones with the boys, or the other way round. A specific conclusion might be that the way a teacher handled a particular confrontation with a child who had misbehaved had been positive or negative.
7 Does anything need to be done to make relationships in this particular classroom better?

ACTIVITY 14

Use the 'critical events' approach to help you analyse the relationships in a classroom.

Teasing or tormenting – what should the teacher do?

Observation sheet – Personal relationships

A What led up to the event?

D Interview with teacher

B What happened and who was involved?

E Interview with pupil(s) (if agreed)

C What was the outcome?

F Conclusions

REWARDS AND PUNISHMENTS

Just as the law requires teachers to act as a responsible parent does, so too does it give certain powers to teachers to exercise control or discharge responsibilities. The form of punishments in particular in a school must be approved by the governors and is actually governed by the law, which decrees that punishments must be 'reasonable', defined by one judge as:

- moderate
- not dictated by bad motives
- such as is usual in the school
- such as the parent of the child might expect it to receive if it had done wrong.

This certainly rules out racks and thumbscrews, and the 1986 Education Act made corporal punishment illegal in maintained schools. This ban applies not just to forms of corporal punishment, such as caning and slippering, but also to a 'clip round the ear', which in any case was a potentially dangerous punishment.

Rewards are one of two principal kinds:

extrinsic getting a star, a badge, a trophy, a prize, a privilege, something external, often visible, bestowed on behalf of the school or by the teacher.

intrinsic satisfying one's curiosity, a glow of pride from a job well done, something coming more from within the individual.

It is too easy to stereotype rewards and punishments as 'good' or 'bad'. For example, it would be simple to assume that rewards themselves are invariably a good thing and punishments a bad thing, yet a reward out of all proportion to whatever deed earned it, or a minor punishment that was fair and timely and, in retrospect, appreciated by the recipient as having had a positive effect, can soon reverse these simple labels. Similarly, it might be assumed that extrinsic rewards are crude bribes and that intrinsic rewards are the only things worth striving for, but some people need external recognition so that they can set their own standards for themselves. What is often much more important is the effect of rewards and punishments on the children concerned, whether the punishment was unfair, something greatly resented by children, or whether they had earned the reward for their own

efforts. This incident, observed in a class of 10-year-olds, shows how a teacher involved the children themselves in a matter of rewards.

Children who do well in Loamshire Primary School can earn house points. Mrs Everett is pleased with Patricia's work so she awards her two house points. As this is announced to Patricia, other children express disagreement.

Jason	That's not fair, she shouldn't get that many points.
Mrs Everett	All right. I'll give you one point then, Patricia. Are you all happy with that decision?
Elspeth	No, it's still not fair.
Mrs Everett	Well, can anybody suggest a way that we can overcome the problem?
Stephen	Give everybody a point.
Sally	No, that's silly. Don't give Patricia a point at all.
Mary	Give her a star instead. It's worth a star, but not house points.
Mrs Everett	All those that agree with Mary's suggestion put up your hands. Right, that's virtually everybody. Are you happy with that decision, Patricia?

Patricia nods, smiles and seems to the observer to be pleased.

Different teachers have differing responses to this event. Some will say that, if a rewards system is in operation, it should involve the class and not just be imposed. Others, however, argue that in this event rewards were made too important, that children should not just compete for stars and points, but rather learn to accept intrinsic rewards.

 ACTIVITY 15

Look at the use of rewards and punishments in your school, remembering some of the more subtle ones like smiles, nods, using pupils' ideas, withholding attention or recognition, displaying children's work. Record some of these at both school and classroom level in the grid on page 36. If you see more than one teacher, look for similarities and differences.

REWARDS	PUNISHMENTS
At school level	*At school level*
Public signs of reward – what does the school value? Pupils' work on display? Children made monitors? Academic success rewarded? Social behaviour rewarded?	What is the school policy on punishment? What is permitted? Detention? Extra work? What is regarded as mild misbehaviour and what as more serious?
At classroom level	*At classroom level*
Look at teachers' use of rewards. Note the public ones but also smiles, nods, use of praise, encouragement.	Make notes about any punishments you see, either formal or less obvious. Look for sanctions such as loss of privilege, change of seat, sending out of class or to head, reprimands.

SKILLS, STRATEGIES AND DECISION-MAKING

There is no single skill involved when teachers manage classes. What competent practitioners do is bring together a whole repertoire of related skills. These include the ability to prepare and plan; to choose or allow children to select topics and classwork that engage pupils and help them to learn; to use time and space effectively; to be vigilant and aware of what is happening in what may be a scattered, or unevenly shaped working area; to make intelligent decisions in the light of context cues, often involving the rapid scanning of numerous messages; to handle deviancy and disruption; to establish good relationships and a set of rules and conventions that enhance orderly working and learning; to handle resources skilfully; to recognize and understand the wider constituency (including fellow teachers, the head, governors, parents, the local community) within which class management takes place.

Some of these skills have already been dealt with in this workbook, and those such as the management of lesson content are covered in other books in the series, on questioning and explaining, for example. Teaching skills need to be seen as a coherent whole rather than a discrete set of separate and unrelated competencies and techniques, and professional skills in a job like teaching can only be truly enhanced if teachers reflect on questions of value, asking 'Why?' as well as 'How?' or 'What?' In this unit we shall concentrate on the important matter of the effective management of time and space, as well as on some of the specific skills that need to be nurtured and developed when teachers make decisions in classrooms.

In Unit 1 we addressed the question of what constituted skilful class management and what were your own perceptions and those of any group of colleagues, students or teachers with whom you work.

Once you are clearer in your mind about your own beliefs and intentions, it is possible to consider certain specific aspects of class management in more detail. The cluster of related skills needed to manage a class of children in an effective manner includes the intelligent use of time and space.

MANAGING GROUPS AND INDIVIDUALS

The matter of group work is dealt with much more fully in the companion book in this series, *Talking and Learning in Groups* (Dunne and Bennett). However, one of the important strategic decisions teachers make about the management of time and space is whether to use whole class teaching, group work, individual assignments or a combination of these.

Let us suppose, for example, that the teacher intends the children to make a local radio news programme. The children are to collect 'stories', as if they were reporters, and then compile a five-minute bulletin, tape record it, and finally play it back to the rest of the class. She might then make the following strategic decisions:

Whole class teaching At the beginning of the lesson, to set the scene, ask about 'news', what it is, why events are newsworthy, how news programmes are assembled (important stories first, newsreader plus interviews or on-the-spot reporters, etc.). Then, to explain how the class will be split into news teams of five pupils, discuss how they might organize things, what they are to do, how they will tape record their bulletin. In the middle of the session, she might bring the whole class together to review progress, answer questions, solve problems. At the end, the whole class might listen to the bulletins, discuss choice of items, priorities, delivery, succinctness, information value.

Group work   After the beginning, groups of five work out their stories, discuss ideas, choose who should be reporters, who will actually read the news, who will do sound effects, pretend to be a member of the public being interviewed, etc.

Individual work   Digging out information, writing a short script for a 30 second item, practising using the tape recorder, reading the bulletin.

You might like to make a list of possible circumstances in which whole class teaching, group work and individual assignments appear to make good sense, of what advantages and disadvantages each might offer teachers and pupils, and of the management concerns in each case. For example, you might speculate that during whole class teaching, control of behaviour might be easier if pupils are engaged, but harder if the more able and less able have lost interest; that it will take a great deal of effort to monitor effectively during individual assignment work; that managing groups doing different activities might involve more detailed preparation and extra mobility and vigilance. You can then test your own hypotheses against your experience in the classroom-based activities below and above.

THE MANAGEMENT OF TIME

In the context of classroom learning, the use of time is an important matter. There is often a limited amount of time available and skilful use of it can be the difference between children learning effectively and learning little. Teachers' sharing out of their own time – between planning and preparing, marking children's work, asking questions, giving information, listening to and talking with individuals or group, or taking part in extra-curricular activities – is well worthy of scrutiny.

Anyone wishing to manage time effectively would find that some kind of occasional systematic analysis can be quite illuminating. For example, it is possible to attempt to record each hour a breakdown of how the previous hour has been spent. A series of headings can be assembled, such as 'planning and preparation', 'teaching children', 'attending formal or informal meetings', 'marking work' and 'assessing progress', 'social time' and the ubiquitous 'other'. Every hour the teacher can make

a very quick and rough estimate of how many minutes were spent in each of the categories. It is then possible, at the end of a day or a week, to see how one's time has been spent.

Indeed, it is easy to be shocked at how much time has been devoted to meetings, how little time spent on teaching, or how much time assessment may take during certain periods of the school year. Though the exercise in itself consumes precious time, it is worth doing, on an occasional basis, especially when teachers are seeking to redirect their energies.

The main purpose of this section, however, is not to consider these broader issues, but rather to look specifically at time spent by children on the task in hand. The notion of 'time on task' is one which has received considerable attention during the last few years. One operational definition of the important concept of 'motivation' is 'the amount of time and the degree of arousal or attentiveness brought to a task or activity'.

Take as an example the game of chess. If you are not 'motivated' to play chess then you will give it little time or attention and probably, therefore, not play the game especially well. If, on the other hand, you are highly 'motivated', then you may well belong to a chess club, read books on chess, spend time on the chess column in your newspaper (rather than pass over it, as most readers do), perhaps even carry a pocket chess set around so that you can play through games you come across or play against other enthusiasts. In other words, you will devote a great deal of time in a psychologically aroused state to the game of chess and, as a result, you will probably be a better player than you would have been had you not been 'motivated'. Spending more time on something does not guarantee better learning, but it can certainly make a valuable contribution to it.

Time in itself, however, is an empty concept. If someone spends hours copying out telephone directories, then little of value will be learned. There are two highly significant features of time spent on the task that are essential requirements if effective learning is to take place. The first is that the time be spent on something *worthwhile*, and the second is that there should be some *degree of success* by the pupil. If children were to spend a great deal of time, for example, writing down incorrect answers to arithmetical problems or constantly misspelling the same word, then they would actually be learning errors, and, once established, such errors are difficult to unlearn. Hence the need for careful scrutiny of the kind of activity that takes place, not merely of the amount of time spent on it.

In the research we carried out during the

Pupil	Seconds on task (out of 20)			Level of deviancy		
	Low (0–6)	Medium (7–13)	High (14–20)	None	Mild	More Serious
1 Mary			✓	✓		
2 John		✓			✓	
3 Alice	✓					✓

Leverhulme Primary Project we observed several hundred lessons, in which we spent part of the time observing every single individual child in the class. One approach we used was to study each child for 20 seconds and then make two decisions. The first was to ask whether children appeared to be 'high' (14–20 seconds), 'medium' (7–13 seconds) or 'low' (0–6 seconds), in terms of on-task behaviour, that is spending time on whatever they were supposed to be doing. The second was to record whether children were behaving well during that 20-second period or were mildly or seriously deviant. Mild deviance involved such matters as illicit chatter, movement, interfering with the work of another child, and more serious deviance included physical aggression, vandalism or damage to property, or verbal or non-verbal behaviour significantly insulting to another child or the teacher.

In order to record these two pieces of information, researchers completed a grid as shown below. Supposing Mary had worked consistently and behaved well, John had worked for about half the 20 seconds and spent the rest distracting his neighbour, and Alice had not appeared to be involved in the task at all and had called the teacher an 'old cow'. The resulting grid would have looked like the above (though in real life it is not always so symmetrical, as pupils may be low on task but well behaved, for example).

Often it will seem crystal clear to the observer whether a pupil is engaged in the task or not and similarly whether or not a pupil is misbehaving, but on some occasions it will be unclear. It can be extremely difficult to decide whether someone who is staring intently into space is daydreaming or planning his next move, and, indeed, whether the daydreaming itself is an important part of learning, allowing someone a brief respite before the next intensive bout of work. Thus, any recordings of this kind are merely rough-and-ready estimates, valuable when taken into consideration alongside other evidence, but not in themselves flawless indicators of types of behaviour and successful learning.

ACTIVITY 16

You can use a data sheet like the one shown above to assemble a general picture of involvement in the task and misbehaviour in a class you observe. It is not usually possible to teach and conduct the exercise on your own class at the same time. The observer needs to be free to observe as accurately as possible and the teacher needs to be able to teach without the inhibition of having to record systematically. You will need to find someone able to observe your teaching, therefore, if you wish to have this sort of analysis of it. Unfortunately, too little time is made available for teachers to observe each other teach, but this is the sort of valuable exercise that can be done by two teachers working together on their own staff development programme, by two students in the same school for teaching practice, or by a student and a teacher sharing a class.

Method   Complete the data sheet on page 41, observing each pupil for 20 seconds and then for each pupil, inserting one tick to indicate seconds on task and another to indicate level of deviancy. Cover each pupil in the class and either do the exercise in a systematic manner, observing each table or each section of the room in turn, or, if you know the pupils' names, in a random way, making sure you do not observe the same child twice. Make the best decision you can in each case. Also ensure the observations are done in a discreet and sensitive manner, from a suitable vantage point.

Calculate an involvement and a deviancy score for the lesson using the following procedure.

Involvement score (possible range 0–100)

First of all you must obtain Factor A. To do this you multiply the total number of pupils in the 'low' category by 0, the total number of pupils in the 'medium' category by 1 and the total in the 'high' category by 2, and add the resulting scores. Suppose you observe 28 pupils and find 2, 10 and 16 pupils to be 'low,', 'medium' and 'high' on task respectively, then Factor A would be as follows:

'Low' on task	2 pupils	Multiplied by 0 =	0
'Medium' on task	10 pupils	Multiplied by 1 =	10
'High' on task	16 pupils	Multiplied by 2 =	32
TOTAL	28 pupils	FACTOR A =	42

Next, insert Factor A in the equation below:

$$\text{Involvement score} = \frac{\text{Factor A}}{\text{Total no of pupils} \times 2} = \frac{42}{28 \times 2} = \frac{42}{56} = 0.75$$

Finally, multiply by 100, giving an Involvement score of 75. If every child were fully involved the maximum score would be 100, and if no-one were involved in the task the minimum score would be 0. The maximum of 100 would be obtained if all the pulpils in the class were observed to be 'high' on task.

Deviancy score

Exactly the same procedure is adopted, but this time the 'none' category is multiplied by 0, the 'mild' is multiplied by 1 and the 'more serious' is multiplied by 2. Thus the following distribution would produce a deviancy score of 20 if there were 25 pupils in the class, and 16, 8 and one pupil were in the 'none', 'mild' and 'more serious' categories respectively.

'None'	= 16 pupils	multiplied by 0 =	0
'Mild'	= 8 pupils	multiplied by 1 =	8
'More serious'	= 1 pupil	multiplied by 2 =	2
TOTAL	25 pupils	FACTOR A =	10

$$\text{Deviancy score} = \frac{\text{Factor A}}{\text{Total no of pupils} \times 2} = \frac{10}{25 \times 2} = \frac{10}{50} = 0.20$$

This score of 0.20 multiplied by 100 then gives a Deviancy score of 20.

Discussion of the observation between the teacher and the observer can cover such points as:

- What is the general level of involvement and why is the picture as it is?
- What is the general level of good behaviour/misbehaviour and what sort of misbehaviour takes place?
- Which children behave in what manner? Give

attention to each child if possible, not just to those who misbehave or work intensively.

- Is the observed behaviour typical (it is wise to do more than one such observation with a class).
- Discuss some of the events the observer witnessed, both positive and negative kinds. Observations can be compiled by the recording of critical events (see Activity 14).

Consider ways of increasing involvement and reducing misbehaviour.

This involves addressing such matters as:

- Was/were the assignment(s) suitable and worthwhile?
- Had the ground been prepared sufficiently, so that pupils were clear what they had to do?
- Was the teacher's use of his/her own time effectively managed or was the setting up and/or development of the lesson too protracted, slow, or tedious?
- Did the teacher monitor pupils' work and behaviour?
- Was misbehaviour handled effectively and was good behaviour properly acknowledged?
- What happened when pupils finished their work?
- Were pupils able to work independently if this was what was required, or were they too reliant on the teacher?
- Was the achievement of individual children satisfactory, given the time available? (It is sometimes worth choosing six 'target' pupils, three boys and three girls, a boy and a girl from among each of high, medium and low ability pupils, and looking specifically at what they achieved during the observation period.)

In an observation period it is sometimes possible to conduct more than one such 'circuit' of the class. If this is done, then involvement and deviancy levels can be calculated for different kinds of activity. Questions to be asked include:

- Were there significant looking differences in pattern for different kinds of activity?
- What kinds of activity secured highest involvement and lowest misbehaviour?
- Was there more misbehaviour when certain things happened? (For example, it sometimes happens that deviancy increases during *transitions* from one activity to another, especially if movement and jostling occur).
- Were there significant differences?

As a result, the teacher and observer can discuss any difficult moments and find ways of managing more effectively in future potential problems.

INDIVIDUAL PUPIL OBSERVATION

Teacher: _____ Date: _____ Lesson: _____

Pupil	Seconds on task (out of 20)			Level of deviancy		
	Low 0–6	Medium 7–13	High 14–20	None	Mild	More serious
1						
2						
3						
4						
5						
6						
7						
8						
9						
10						
11						
12						
13						
14						
15						
16						
17						
18						
19						
20						
21						
22						
23						
24						
25						
26						
27						
28						
29						
30						
31						
32						
33						
34						
35						
Total						
	× 0	× 1	× 2	× 0	× 1	× 2
Factor A	0			0		
Sum						

Formula $\dfrac{\text{Sum of Factor A}}{\text{Total of Pupils} \times 2} \times 100$ = Involvement or Deviancy level

Task   Involvement level _____

Deviancy level _____

During the Leverhulme Primary Project we observed hundreds of lessons using this approach. There was considerable variety in the scores obtained and in the critical events analysed. A summary of some findings based on one project involving more than 200 lessons given by students and experienced teachers is shown below.

	Involvement score	Deviancy score
Average of whole group	71	5
Lowest average for any individual teacher	38	0
Lowest score for any individual lesson	28	0
Highest average for any individual teacher	92	20
Highest score for any individual lesson	100	26

Great caution must be exercised when comparing scores with these group figures. Involvement and deviancy scores are *not measures of quality*. They are rough-and-ready estimates of attentiveness to the task. It would be possible to obtain a high involvement and low deviancy score by terrorizing pupils into copying out telephone directories, but the educational value would be zero. Some of the above figures represent lessons with small orderly classes, and others are of teachers with large classes in inner city schools working with extremely difficult pupils. Qualitative aspects, such as the nature of the group, the size of the class, the available materials, equipment, furnishings and extra adult ancillary help, will all affect behaviour and concentration. Other aspects of time, such as the amount of time teachers allow between asking a question and a pupil's answering, are dealt with elsewhere in this series, for example, in the volumes on questioning and explaining.

Ineffective use of space – children too near the sink

THE MANAGEMENT OF SPACE

It is equally illuminating to study the use of space in a classroom. Consider the following two examples.

Example 1   Floating and sinking

A group of 7-year-olds is at work in a small rectangular-shaped classroom. Along the wall with the windows is a sink. One-third of the class is told to do work on the subject 'What floats and what sinks?' while the other two-thirds carry on with their normal work. Later, this two-thirds will have their turn at this activity. Working in pairs, each pair is told to collect a small plastic tank and half fill it with water from the sink. They must then return to their place and put various objects, a cork, an apple, a stone, some sand, a rubber ball, etc., into the water and record whether each floated or sank. Unfortunately, however, the children carrying the water have to pick their way past others seated around tables near the sink. The escape route from the sink is narrow, there are bags and coats on the floor, and several pupils splash water as they pick their way back to their seats, resulting in much grumbling from other pupils.

Example 2   Being able to see

The teacher is trying to explain to a group of 8-year-olds that they will be going on a field trip the following day. She has drawn a map on the blackboard showing some of the features they will see on their visit. All pupils are sitting around hexagonal-shaped tables. Those with their backs to the teacher crane their necks to see the board, others half stand to look at the map as the teacher explains. There are various comments from the children, like, 'I can't see, Janet' or 'Move your head, Ian.'

In both these examples it was the ineffective use of space that led to problems. In the first one, failure to clear a space for children to get to and from the sink, or failure to arrange the class's activities in such a way that the 'wet' work was done as near the sink as possible, produced friction between pupils engaged in different kinds of activity. In the second example, sitting around hexagonal tables was fine for most of the class's activities, but when they all had to look at the blackboard and the teacher, some kind of modification was needed so that all could see properly, like turning round their chairs or gathering on the floor space near the blackboard.

Many teachers work in classrooms that are less than ideal, so the best has to be made of what is available. However, it is worth thinking carefully about how to use space at your disposal. In our own home, we may, if we are lucky, be able to spend a great deal of time designing a kitchen, deciding exactly where the cooker and washer should go, whether one can squeeze in a dining corner, and thinking about the kinds of activities that will go on and how they can best be accommodated. Time spent planning a classroom layout, given the amount of time spent there, will be a wise investment.

ACTIVITY 17

Using a piece of squared paper, design a classroom layout with a particular class in mind: it might be one you are currently teaching, have recently taught or one you imagine you might have to teach in future. You should make the following assumptions:

- You have about 52 square metres (m^2) available.
- There will be anything from 24 to 30 children present at any one time.
- A child sitting at a single desk or table would need about 1 to 1.25 m^2 of floor space.
- Six children sitting round a circular table would need 4 to 5 m^2.
- Three children sitting at a rectangular or semi-hexagonal table would need about 2 to 2.5 m^2.
- You will need at least 2 m^2 of teacher's storage space.
- Each square on your plan represents 1 m^2.

You might, therefore, draw a plan of a rectangle or an L-shape, as shown below, (Circular, oval or star-shaped rooms sound interesting, but architects usually quote astronomical building costs for less conventional shapes.)

Many schools are, of course, designed in a more open-plan manner, with paired classrooms, and shared resources and activity areas. If you wish to design something along these lines, then simply assume that part or all of the walls could be removed so you could simply design your own homebase part of the unit. Next, you should draw into the squared paper your layout showing where children would sit and work, what sort of facilities you would like and where these might be located. When you have completed your sketch, make a list of what resources and facilities you would like to see in an adjacent additional 10 m^2 per class of shared resource area, available to each teacher.

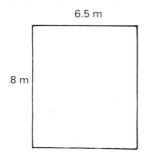

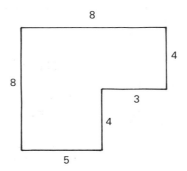

Possible classroom shapes (for Activity 17)

" YES, I SUPPOSE I'VE BEEN TEACHING ABOUT
THIRTY YEARS NOW. "

Finally, you can look critically at your plan and see if it fits as effectively as possible your preferred ways of working. For example, will it allow:

- freedom of movement when required for yourself and children;
- children to work together or alone in a variety of assignments;
- you to address the whole class when necessary;
- proper display of work;
- flexibility to vary activities from day to day or lesson to lesson, with minimum disruption.

In addition, you can try to identify possible problems of management: for example, where excessive and difficult movement might occur as children walk from their chair to some facility they need; whether you would be able to see all that went on, or if there might be blind spots; how you would deal with children working in the working shared-resource area (e.g. what the rules would be, whether permission would be required to go there or if the children would have to report back, how you would keep in touch with what was happening in the area). Finally, you can consider how close you can make your own classroom to your 'ideal' working area,

whether the layout of your room enhances or hinders pupil learning and whether best use is being made of floor space.

VIGILANCE

In order to see what is happening in what may sometimes be a large or irregular shaped area, skilful teachers develop what Jacob Kounin called 'withitness': that is, the ability to split your attention between the individual or group you are with and the rest of the class, to 'have eyes in the back of your head'. This involves two kinds of use of the eyes: the first is the ability to engage pupils in eye-contact, in other words to use your own eyes to look at theirs, for eyes are most important for giving as well as receiving messages; the second is to be able to sweep the classroom rapidly to take in what is happening in various parts of the working area. Exactly the same applies outside the classroom, in a hall or outdoors, for example, and can be vital for such matters as safety, especially on a field trip or during a swimming lesson.

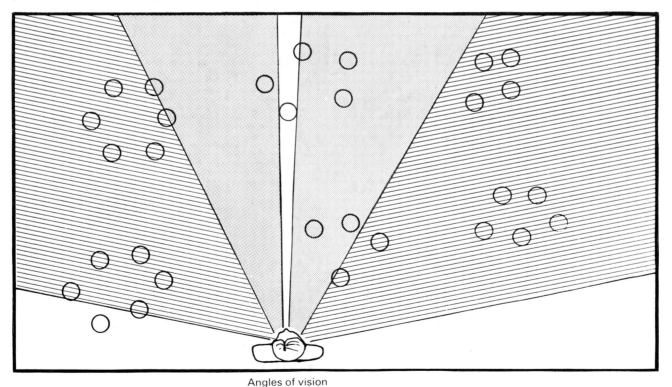

Angles of vision

Key ☐ = in sharp focus   ▨ = in reasonably sharp focus   ▨ = in less sharp focus

Figure 5.1 **Angles of vision**

In order to see the workings of this process of scanning and eye-contact, it is necessary to understand how the human eye works. Figure 5.1 (p. 45) shows three angles, as seen by our eyes. Only a very small area, about 2 to 3 degrees, is seen in very sharp focus, but we have an *awareness* of nearly 180 degrees. As a result, when a teacher looks across a classroom, a V-shaped wedge of about 30–45 degrees is in reasonably sharp focus.

The effect of this is shown in the two pictures opposite. In picture A, small zones are highlighted. This shows approximately the area that is in very sharp focus when a teacher looks across a room: it may be a single face, a picture, a clock, but the actual area is quite small. Picture B, on the other hand, shows the three zones together, a central two to three degrees are in very sharp focus, a 45-degree area in reasonably sharp focus and the rest of the 170- to 180-degree zone in more fuzzy 'awareness' form.

The effect of all this is quite clear, especially where classroom interaction is concerned. For example, it has often been observed that teachers' questions may be largely directed into that V-shaped 45-degree wedge in front of them. Thus teachers who always teach from near their desk or at the blackboard may find that most of their questions are addressed to or answered by children in central positions, and that those sitting near the edge of the room are less frequently involved. Since children understand perfectly well the dynamics of classroom life, those who want to be in the 'busy traffic' area often head for seats or tables in central locations, those seeking a quieter environment may choose the periphery and seats or tables by walls and windows, and it is not unknown for those who disrupt to choose the corners furthest away from the teacher's desk.

Vigilance is not, however, something that should be undertaken in isolation. These photographs show some common situations in which vigilance and effective use of eyes can pay off.

Anticipating problems

The teacher notices that children at one table have finished early and are beginning to distract others.

Monitoring work

Walking round the class involves more than just creating a draught. Teachers who monitor children's work effectively during class time have a clear picture about children's learning.

Public audit

'Ian, I'm hoping you'll have done all those sums

Anticipating problems

Monitoring work

Public audit

PICTURE A

PICTURE B

Avoiding accidents

Personal and social education

when I come over to you. Amanda and Sally, have you finished preparing assembly?' An occasional audit signals that the teacher knows what is happening, but if too frequent children are interrupted unnecessarily.

Avoiding accidents

Design and technology sessions can be absorbing and exciting, but safety is an important matter as well.

Personal and social education

Are children helping each other, sharing, waiting their turn, or are they behaving negatively, belittling each other, showing meanness?

CONTEXT CUES

Trainee teachers sometimes ask, 'What do you do if . . .?' questions, and are then disappointed when teachers or tutors reply, 'It depends on the circumstances.' Teaching would be a much easier occupation if all events within certain categories were identical. Yet classrooms are unlike factory production lines where robots can insert rivets in precisely the same place, with precisely the same effect, for week upon week.

a ACTIVITY 18

Incident

A student teacher, new to her teaching practice school, suddenly finds David, a 10-year-old pupil from another class, walking into her lesson, and crossing the room between herself and a group of pupils she is addressing. She is a little taken aback at the intrusion of this stranger, and is not certain how to react.

1 Consider just a few of the countless possible context factors, of which she might or might not be aware, and reflect on how each might affect her reaction.
   (a) The school is open plan and freedom of movement is permitted, even encouraged.
   (b) David is known as a regular trouble-maker who goes to other parts of the school and causes disruption.
   (c) David's father is seriously ill in hospital and David is upset and confused.
   (d) The head has sent David round the school with a message.
   (e) David is very tall for his age.
   (f) David is very small for his age.
   (g) The teacher and children are working with potentially dangerous technology equipment.

(h) The class laughs uproariously.
(i) The class goes completely silent.
(j) David is a child who has been statemented as having learning difficulties and easily becoming confused.

2 Think of other context cues that might influence a teacher's decision and discuss how, in each case, the teacher's reaction to the incident could or should be affected.

DEVIANCY AND DISRUPTION

If you have completed Activity 16 (see p. 39) and observed individual pupils one by one, you will have noted different kinds of deviancy or disruption. Definitions of deviancy do, of course, vary. For some teachers, any kind of talking to another pupil might constitute naughty or deviant behaviour; for others, talk might be permitted provided it is related to the task in hand; yet others might tolerate quite a high level of social chat.

Our studies of classrooms during the Leverhulme Project showed that most misbehaviour in primary classrooms was of a minor, if irritating kind, primarily related to over-noisy talk (as was found in similar studies of secondary schools; see Wragg 1984). In one study of more than 200 lessons, the most common source of deviant behaviour was indeed excessively noisy talk, followed by misdemeanours connected with movement (leaving seat without permission, running) and, thirdly, inappropriate use of materials (flicking someone with ruler or pencil, making paper aeroplane). In more than 94 per cent of cases teachers made some response before the deviance escalated, most commonly an order to cease and/or a reprimand. In two-thirds of cases a pupil was named and in 90 per cent of cases the target of the reprimand was judged to be correct. More serious matters, like physical aggression to another pupil and insults to the teacher, were only recorded in one or two per cent of the lesson segments analysed.

The Elton Report (DES 1989), a government-sponsored enquiry into discipline in schools, reported questionnaire responses that were very similar to our lesson observations. A survey by Sheffield University for the Elton Committee found that primary teachers reported children talking noisily or out of turn, distracting others, and inappropriate use of materials, as the most frequent occurrences they had to deal with. The Elton Report concluded:

 Our recommendations relate to a whole range of discipline problems, particularly persistent disruption. We found that most schools are on the whole well ordered. But even in well run schools minor disruption appears to be a problem. The relatively trivial incidents which most concern teachers make it harder for teachers to teach and pupils to learn.

Nevertheless, even though relatively little serious misbehaviour has been noted in live studies of primary classrooms, there are two important matters that need to be addressed. The first is what to do about such matters as noise levels, the second is how to handle the more serious forms of misbehaviour when they occur. In the case of dealing with noise in the classroom, reflect on the following reactions by teachers observed during the Leverhulme Project.

(a) 'I've asked you to be quiet and I can see (pointing) 1, 2, 3 . . . 4, 5 . . . 6, 7 children who're making too much noise. Quieten it down.' Class works more quietly.
(b) Children are balancing building bricks on scales at one table. There is considerable noise and a boy is hitting a girl at the same table. She moves to another table protesting. He then hits another girl at the same table. She goes over to the teacher and asks her to tie her apron. The noise from the far end of the room continues, but the teacher does not intervene.
(c) (During a story, 5-year-olds sitting on the carpet) 'Carina, I've asked you to stop talking. Come and sit here at the front next to me.' Child sits by teacher and becomes more interested in story.
(d) A student teacher tries to give out worksheets to 7–8-year-olds amid growing noise. She asks for quiet and then stamps her foot. It has no effect on the noise. In interview afterwards she describes stamping her foot as 'Stupid . . . they'll only copy you, so I don't think I'll do that again.'

Responses (a) and (c) were effective in stopping the noise, but the teacher's failure to respond in (b) and the student teacher's foot stamping were not. Like other forms of misbehaviour, excessively noisy talk can result from different causes. In some cases it is the lack of agreed rules that lead children to 'test the limits'. If rules have not been defined, then children may seek a definition by raising the noise until the teacher signals it is too high. Teachers who were effective at controlling the noise level had often clarified the limits very early in their first lessons with their class.

𝑎 ACTIVITY 19

We put a number of discipline situations to teachers in the form of photographs, some illustrating a more serious problem.

1 Consider the two pictures A and B and the story lines that go with them. Picture A shows two children pushing each other, Picture B a confrontation with a girl pupil.

2 Decide in each case what you would do if this happened in your own class.

Picture A You're sitting with your back to this group when you hear a noise. You turn around and see two children messing about. You have told them off once that day for not getting on with their work. What, if anything, do you do?

Picture B You have caught this girl scribbling on someone else's book. You have told her off in front of the class and you hear her mutter 'old cow' under her breath. The children nearby snigger. What, if anything, do you do?

3 Consider and discuss the responses of teachers in interview. The replies are given in descending order of frequency, so that the first answer is the one most often given.

Picture A

1 Separate the two children.
2 Find out what has happened.
3 It would depend on the children/their expectations/school sanctions.
4 Look at the task the children are supposed to be doing and reassess it and the situation.
5 Tell them off/comment on their behaviour.
6 See it as time wasting and so get them back to work.
7 Punish them (most frequent suggestion – keep them in).

PICTURE A – Messing about

PICTURE B – 'Old cow'

Other mentions – sit next to teacher, bring them out, talk individually to them.

Picture B

1 Speak to her on her own, now or later.
2 Show emotion – anger, sorrow, upset, humour.
3 It would depend on the child.
4 Send to the head.
5 Involve the whole class in some way.
6 Punish the girl.
7 Ask her to repeat it.
8 Tell her off.

Other mentions – withdraw her, get her to rub out the scribbling.

4 Discuss how teachers should deal with more serious examples of misbehaviour. Consider the following:

(a) Seeing a child on his/her own after the lesson or at break and what *safeguards* might be needed for both the teacher and the child (e.g. overawing young child, need for a witness)

(b) When parents would need to be involved (when does a routine matter become more serious, for example, or what constitutes behaviour so unacceptable, or so worrying, that parents must be involved).

(c) When governors, particularly the chairman, should be involved, for example, in the case of a pupil being excluded (what used to be called 'suspension'). Remember that governors have responsibility for discipline in the school, even if it is the head and teachers who are responsible for the day-to-day handling of discipline matters. It is, however, the governors who decide on exclusions, not the teachers, even though teachers may make recommendations. Also the local authority must be notified, particularly if the exclusion is for more than five days. Furthermore, parents may appeal and, if they wish, governors may in turn appeal to the local authority, if they are not happy with the LEA's decision (see *A Handbook for School Governors* by E.C. Wragg and J.A. Partington).

(d) What use might be made of any facilities available outside the school, such as a special unit for disruptive pupils or the help of an educational psychologist.

(e) What 'low key' methods can be used inside the school, like the use of 'time out' (a spell outside the class, say, with the head or another teacher, to 'cool down').

(f) Whether the misbehaving child is being overwhelmed by several adults, possibly behaving in contradictory ways.

DEVELOPING AND ENHANCING COMPETENCE

A WHOLE SCHOOL APPROACH

It is extremely valuable for teachers to review their approach to class management in a systematic way. It is even more valuable if all the teachers in the same school discuss their class management, not with a view to becoming clones of each other, but so that the kinds of inconsistencies that can confuse children or cause problems can at least be considered openly.

There are also roles for the whole community. Just as teachers need to consider how they manage time, resources and space, what sort of rules and relationships have been established in their classes or what to do about disorderly behaviour, so too do children need to learn to take responsibility, make decisions, organize themselves effectively and also to control their own behaviour. Furthermore, parents need to be included in the process, as do governors, since they are responsible for staff appointments and for school policy. Dinner helpers and ancillaries need to be aware of school policy also, and rules and conventions should apply in the playground, dining areas, circulation space and cloakrooms, not just in classrooms, although there may be some differences.

The Elton Report (DES 1989) was concerned mainly with school discipline, but its recommendation about the way ahead would apply equally to other aspects of class management:

> We recommend that headteachers and their senior management teams should take the lead in developing school plans for promoting good behaviour. Such plans should ensure that the school's code of conduct and the values represented in its formal and informal curricula reinforce one another; promote the highest possible degree of consensus about standards of behaviour among staff, pupils and parents; provide clear guidance to all three groups about these standards and their practical application; and encourage staff to recognise and praise good behaviour as well as dealing with bad behaviour.

One way of raising issues is to begin with consideration of hypothetical events rather than those that have actually happened within the school. It is sometimes easier to do this without prejudice, recrimination or blame being attached. For example, take the case of bullying, something that can happen quite suddenly even in the best-run school. If teachers begin by reviewing a case that has actually happened recently in their own school, then the head and teacher concerned may feel defensive, if their actions are under scrutiny, and it may be difficult to discuss policy separately from personalities. Activity 20 is based on an actual letter sent by a parent to the head of a primary school.

ACTIVITY 20

1 Consider this letter, which was written by the parent of an 8-year-old boy to the head of his primary school.

Dear Mr X,

I have thought long and hard before writing this letter, but I should like to come and see you about my son Michael who is being bullied regularly by two boys in his class. The reason I have not contacted you before is because Michael has begged me not to say anything, as he does not want to make things worse, and he is frightened that one of the boys in particular will take revenge on him.

The two boys are Ian Jenkins and Andrew Wilson, and Ian Jenkins is much worse than Andrew. In lessons they often tease Michael. Ian Jenkins hid his ruler the other day and Andrew Wilson wrote on his new bag. It is usually petty things in the classroom, but outside is much worse. They often pick on him in the yard at playtime and that is why he has started coming home for lunch. They have told him that they are going to 'get him' after school, and one night they chased him down the whole length of Brook Street and he had to run all the way home. I know it sounds silly, but he was terrified when Ian Jenkins said he was going to get a big knife and cut his liver out.

Yesterday was the final straw. Michael came home and told me that Ian Jenkins wanted him to give him 50p or he would beat him up. That is why I have kept Michael at home today. I should like to come and see you as soon as possible, but please do not say anything to the two boys. I dare not tell Michael I have written to you and when I come to see you I shall have to tell him I am going shopping and leave him at his grandma's.

Yours sincerely

Mrs Elizabeth Gray

2 Consider how the head should react to this letter. In particular consider:

Confidentiality   Mrs Gray asks for confidentiality. Should the head persuade her to let him or the class teacher talk discreetly to the boys concerned?

Class teacher   What should the class teacher do about events said to be happening in the classroom?

Playground   What should be done about events said to be happening in the school grounds?

After school   What should be done about events that happen after school? (Teachers are legally in loco parentis while children are on their journey to or from school).

Parents   Assume that eventually Mrs Gray agrees that the matter may be raised in a discreet way. Should the head see the parents of Ian Jenkins and Andrew Wilson? If not, why not? If yes, for what purpose?

Children   What should the head and class teacher do about the three children involved? What should be done by the head and what by the class teacher?

Should the children be seen separately or together? How should each child's version of events be elicited? What action should be taken if Michael's version of the story is (a) untrue? (b) partly true, but exaggerated? (c) entirely true?

3 Discuss what might be done in your own school to prevent bullying and whether some written code or checklist might need to be drawn up for school staff.

This Activity can also be done in a modified form by governors (they can see and discuss Mrs Gray's letters at a governors' meeting or training conference and consider or review school policy in the light of their discussion) or by parents. If parent groups consider the letter, it is important that they not only imagine they are the parents of Michael Gray, but also the parents of Ian Jenkins. If you are the parent of Michael Gray you may well want immediate retribution and punishment, but if you are the parent of Ian Jenkins you will ask about such matters as whether Michael Gray is telling the truth, whether he has himself been a pest to your son or needled him in some way and whether he exaggerates or fantasizes about events. There are often several aspects and versions of such a story, and it is important to hear them.

Bullying, however, is a serious matter and should always be investigated. My own reaction to the Michael Gray story, if his account turned out to be true, would be to see his parents first; persuade them to let me investigate discreetly with the class teacher and also to talk to Michael; next to talk to Ian and Andrew, first separately and then together; subsequently to confer again with the class teacher to compare all versions of events; to see the parents of Ian and Andrew, not just about the bullying but also about the extortion; to take whatever action then seemed necessary in the light of interviews and discussions; finally to raise the issue of bullying with other children in the school, some time later and in the context of a made-up story about some children in a school in another country and in the context of 'treating other people as you would like to be treated yourself'. It is most important, however, in any guidelines, to make provision to hear different accounts of events. Simply to decide prematurely and without any evidence that the alleged bully is a villain who should be punished, or the alleged victim is a wimp who should be toughened up, is to court disaster.

The question of bullying is an emotive one, but the case study approach can be used to discuss other matters of importance to class management in the school. It is not difficult to invent hypothetical story lines based on real events and then discuss individual and group policy. Here are just four possibilities. It is important to start with a fictional version so that people feel less under the microscope.

1　*Punishment* – Mrs Jones keeps people in at lunchtime if they come into her classroom without permission at break. In the room next door, however, Mr Brown does not mind children coming in so long as they do not mess about. What do you do if teachers' punishment conventions vary? Review the use of punishments in the school.

2　*Rewards* – Mrs Thomas gives stars and points for good work, so some of Mr Jackson's class ask if they can have them. Mr Jackson replies that he does not want to operate that sort of system as children should learn to enjoy doing their work for its own sake. Does it matter if individual teachers have different reward systems?

3　*Resources* – The school's bill for paper and card is increasing. Mr Smith says that the trouble is that some of the newer teachers waste paper, and that

when he was at school during the war he learned the importance of using paper sparingly, because there was not much about. One of the younger teachers says that she does not 'waste' paper and materials, but if you want children to fulfil the sort of curriculum requirements that speak of 'improving a design' or 'redrafting a text', then you are bound to give children a second or third opportunity to better their first effort. Should anything be done?

4　*Noise* – Miss Carter and Mr Jessop are in adjacent classrooms with only a sliding partition between them, which is sometimes open and sometimes closed. The problem is that Miss Carter's area is usually quiet and Mr Jessop's much noisier, with more movement and the babble of voices and scrapping of chairs. Friction between the teachers begins to grow. Should anything be done about it? If not, why not? If yes, who should do what?

TEACHER APPRAISAL AND STAFF DEVELOPMENT

There are numerous ways in which work on class management can be incorporated into both staff

A CONSISTENT WHOLE SCHOOL POLICY IS ESSENTIAL

development and teacher appraisal programmes, for the two should be related, appraisal without development being a pretty arid formula. Among possibilities are the use of some of the Activities in this book, most of which can be translated into action with very little extra resources other than time, some elementary organization and goodwill. Other options include the following:

Microteaching

A technique developed originally at Stanford University whereby small groups of children are taught for 5 or 10 minutes with the teacher concentrating on some particular skill like questioning or explaining. The class can be videotaped, the lesson analysed, and then the teacher can try again with a similar group of children. Using microteaching for the development of class management skills needs bigger groups of children, say at least twelve and possibly a half or even a full class. The teacher can try splitting the class into groups, changing activities during the lesson, etc., and the observer or tutor can concentrate on relationships, transitions, instructions, 'withitness' or some other aspect of class management that seems important. The tutor needs to decide whether to let the class behave naturally or to invite one or two pupils to be disruptive.

Film, television and video

There are films such as *Blackboard Jungle* or *To Sir with Love* where a teacher is shown having discipline problems. Although some of the Hollywood endings are not close to real life, there are sometimes particular scenes in certain films which do capture the flavour of a lesson going amiss. Equally, television series such as *Grange Hill* and *Chalkface* can have realistic scenes of school life. Videos, such as the one on 'Teacher Appraisal' in Routledge's Primary Schools' Management Project, contain scenes of misbehaviour in classrooms. Those scenes can be shown and discussed.

Interactive videodisc

Although still in its infancy, the interactive videodisc, with its speedy access to high quality film, can be very useful. There is a shortage of good discs, but the ability to call up scenes of classroom life, look at and discuss them, and then bring on screen further scenes showing the outcomes of the events shown earlier has numerous fruitful

possibilities. The use of bar codes makes for rapid retrieval of the relevant scene, obviating the need to note position numbers of scenes on the disc.

Pictures and slides

There are several pictures in this book and it is not difficult to make colour slides of scenes from classroom life. A still picture is sometimes easier to discuss than moving film.

Literature

There are several accounts of classroom life in novels such as Thomas Mann's *Buddenbrooks* (a class destroying the teacher during registration and roll call), James Joyce's *A Portrait of the Artist as a Young Man* (the prefect of studies flogging pupils for idleness), or Tolstoy's *Yasnaya Polyana* (the silence and orderliness in the lessons of a teacher from a German seminary). Some writers capture the flavour of a lesson more skilfully than any social science textbook, and literary extracts can make excellent discussion material.

Paired learning

One of the most effective ways of improving teachers' or students' professional skills is for them to work in pairs, each taking a turn observing the other teach. Several activities in this book lend themselves to this approach. For example, the teacher observing can note the behaviour of, say, six target pupils and then feed this back to the person teaching, who in turn can do the same for the first teacher. If the focus is on 'vigilance' or 'time on task' or 'personal relationships', not only are valuable pieces of information learned by the observer, but feeding these back to the teacher, who can then reflect and act on practice and professional skill, can lead to a real improvement in class management competence.

A COHERENT VIEW

One very useful exercise for both teachers and student teachers is to set class management firmly into the context of reflection and action across the whole repertoire of teaching skills. On its own, the ability to manage people, resources, time or space is meaningless. Only in a context will techniques and insights acquire value and meaning. This means that class management needs to be seen alongside the other skills that teachers develop, which are covered in other books in this series, like the ability to explain new concepts clearly, to ask different kinds of questions or to listen attentively to what children are saying.

Professional skills should not be dismembered into components that are too tiny. It is quite right to focus on something like class management, or a particular aspect of it like 'vigilance', but it would be foolish to dismantle teaching into molecular particles like 'can hold stick of chalk in right hand' and even more unwise to try to teach competence in this atomized form.

It is worth while for students and teachers in a school to spend some time thinking about the nature of the professional skills they seek to develop in themselves and their colleagues. This may involve many different forms of reflection and action, for professional competence is really made up of intelligent thought translated into intelligent action. One possible approach is to devise a set of headings and sub-headings and consider these. It may be in some hierarchical form, with lower levels and higher levels that can be reached by the more proficient. In class management, for example, a notion like 'organize the handing out and collection of materials' might be a fairly basic matter, involving a teacher thinking about how this can best be organized. Indeed, children themselves could work it out. On the other hand, 'judging the right language register, appropriate response to and suitable activities for a pupil bewildered by a new mathematical or scientific concept' clearly exerts a much higher level of intellectual and practical demand.

At Exeter University, primary trainees assess themselves and are assessed on a set of nine dimensions. These include direct instruction, monitoring, management of order, planning and preparation. In each case there are eight levels through which students can progress, Level 1 being what is expected of beginners and Level 8 being the mark of a competent practitioner. Some examples are:

Level 1

- Distribute provided materials; check children's responses.
- Attempt to operate some procedures for orderly activity.
- Plan basic resources for children working on a given activity.
- Give some account of own performance.

Level 3

- Check clarity of explanation by appropriate questions; convey enthusiasm with appropriate verbal and non-verbal behaviour.
- Use planned and unplanned opportunities to hold conversations with children in order to establish their perspectives; be sensitive to problems of teacher intrusion.
- Continue with attempts to operate in an established formula of rules and procedures.

Level 5

- Provide a programme of guided practice in core areas of the curriculum to suit a range of attainments in class; choose appropriately matched and sequenced practice exercises.
- Experiment with planned conversational teaching on particular aspects of the curriculum.
- Plan a short programme of work to engage a variety of identified skills and intellectual processes and demonstrate attention to transition between activities.
- Offer justifiable explanations of children's response to work; use explanations in practicable ways to plan the next phase of work; show understanding of the diversity of pupils' attainments.

Level 8

- Make explanations efficient and concise; choose examples for their power in the subject.
- Sustain a broad programme of diagnostic teaching.
- Achieve a situation in which order is endemic to the work system.
- Plan for efficiency in use of time and resources with clear reference to the careful management of the teacher's time.

The problem with a hierarchical view is that, by the time we reach the demands of the highest level, the requirements are such that even the most gifted teachers may turn pale, and all of us feel guilty that we do not attain them. Nonetheless, such a mapping exercise does at least clarify what people might aspire to, and the Exeter model is offered as an example, not as a paragon ideal to be copied. It is far more effective if people as a group work out a set of precepts to which they feel committed personally and professionally.

REFERENCES

Bantock, G.H. (1965) *Freedom and Authority in Education*, London: Faber and Faber.

Brown, G.A. and Wragg, E.C. (1993) *Questioning*, London: Routledge.

Buckley, J. (ed.) (1990) *Macmillan School Management Project*, Basingstoke: Macmillan Education (now Routledge).

Buckley, N.K. (1977) *An Ethnographic Study of an Elementary School Teacher's Establishment and Maintenance of Group Norms*. University of Houston, Texas: PhD dissertation, (unpublished).

DES (1989) *Discipline in Schools*, The Elton Report, London: HMSO.

Dunne, E. and Bennett, N. (1990) *Talking and Learning in Groups*, Basingstoke: Macmillan Education (now Routledge).

Duke, D.L. (ed.) (1979) *Classroom Management*, Chicago: National Society for the Study of Education.

Gage, N.L. (1978) *The Scientific Basis of the Art of Teaching*, New York: Teachers College Press.

Gage, N.L. (1985) *Hard Gains in the Soft Sciences*, Bloomington, Ill.: Phi Delta Kappa.

Glasser, W. (1969) *Schools without Failure*, New York: Harper and Row.

Kelly, G.A. (1970) 'A brief introduction to personal construct theory', in D. Bannister (ed.) *New Perspectives in Personal Construct Theory*, London: Academic Press.

King, R.A. (1978) *All Things Bright and Beautiful?* Chichester: Wiley.

Kounin, J.S. (1970) *Discipline and Group Management in Classrooms*, New York: Holt, Rinehart and Winston.

Lewin, K. (1943) 'Psychology and the process of group living', *Journal of Social Psychology* 17: 113–31.

Neill, A.S. (1962) *Summerhill*, London: Victor Gollancz.

Rogers, C.R. (1970) *On Being A Person*, Boston: Houghton Mifflin.

Skinner, B.F. (1968) *The Technology of Teaching*, New York: Appleton-Century-Crofts.

Wragg, E.C. (1974) *Teaching Teaching*, Newton Abbot: David and Charles.

Wragg, E.C. (ed.) (1984) *Classroom Teaching Skills*, London: Croom Helm (now Routledge 1989).

Wragg, E.C. (1987) *Teacher Appraisal*, Basingstoke: Macmillan Education (now Routledge).

Wragg, E.C. and Brown, G.A. (1993) *Explaining*, London: Routledge.

Wragg, E.C. and Partington, J.A. (1980) *A Handbook for School Governors*, London: Routledge.

Some books on class management

Docking, J.W. (1980) *Control and Discipline in Schools*, London: Harper and Row.

Fontana, D. (1985) *Classroom Control*, London: Methuen.

Marland, M. (1975) *The Craft of the Classroom*, London: Heinemann.

Robertson, J. (1981) *Effective Classroom Control*, London: Hodder and Stoughton.